# ALL THINGS JERKY

# ALL THINGS JERKY

## THE DEFINITIVE GUIDE TO MAKING DELICIOUS JERKY AND DRIED SNACK OFFERINGS

### ANDY LIGHTBODY
### KATHY MATTOON

#### FOREWORD BY JIM ZUMBO

Skyhorse Publishing

Skyhorse Publishing books may be purchased in bulk at special discounts for sales promotion, corporate gifts, fund-raising, or educational purposes. Special editions can also be created to specifications. For details, contact the Special Sales Department, Skyhorse Publishing, 307 West 36th Street, 11th Floor, New York, NY 10018 or info@ skyhorsepublishing.com.

Skyhorse® and Skyhorse Publishing® are registered trademarks of Skyhorse Publishing, Inc.®, a Delaware corporation.

Visit our website at www.skyhorsepublishing.com.

10 9 8 7 6 5 4 3

Library of Congress Cataloging-in-Publication Data is available on file.

Cover design by Rain Saukas
Cover photo credit: Thinkstock

Print ISBN: 978-1-63450-489-8
Ebook ISBN: 978-1-5107-0159-5

Printed in China

# ALL THINGS JERKY

# CONTENTS

# FOREWORD

To many of us who live, work, write, and love the out of doors, jerky is not only a delicious treat, but a backpack staple. Making your own jerky meats, birds, and fish, and being able to infuse flavors that are limited only by your imagination is one of the easiest ways to share great eats with family and friends. Just break out a bag of homemade jerky, and it's remarkable just how many *new friends* are guaranteed to show up.

With virtually everyone loving jerky and dehydrated fruits and vegetables, making these snacks at home is a great way to learn new skills. For sportsmen, it's a simple way to clean out leftover meats and fish from the freezer and turn them into something special. For others of us, it's also a great way to relive those special outdoor hunting and fishing experiences, show off some culinary talents, and produce healthy treats that will save us lots of money as compared to purchasing store-bought and commercially produced packages of "*uncertain*" foodstuffs.

If you do a little math, you'll see that over-the-counter jerky actually costs anywhere from $30-$50 a pound, or even more. It's no wonder that jerky and meat snack sales here in the US have grown to be a nearly $3 billion per year industry! But the truth is, it's not only to easy to make at home, but can save you a small fortune if you want good eats and enjoy sharing with your friends. Even if you have to buy your meats at the grocery store, instead of heading to a freezer full of big game, wild poultry/ducks, and fish, the cost for making your snacks is rarely going to be more than $8-$12 a pound. *That, folks, is a lot of great jerky eating for everyone.* Hunt and fish for your own meats, birds, and fish and the savings are going to be even greater, and you're going to be asking yourself *why* you haven't been making all these treats at home a long time ago.

*All Things Jerky* is that all-inclusive book that looks at practically everything that you can process for drying and smoking at home. Whether you are a beginner or a veteran *jerky master,* lifelong outdoor journalists Kathy Mattoon and Andy Lightbody show you just how easy and delicious these home treats can be. If you're a beginner, they show you how to get started and keep it simple. If you think you're already pretty good, this book will make you better!

With home jerky smokers, grills, dehydrators, cures, spices, rubs, marinades, and much more being available at every sporting goods store and all over the Internet, this book profiles all the latest and greatest products, new technologies, tips, secrets, and over one hundred easy-to-follow recipes that they have gathered from friends, jerky masters, and noted outdoor writers/chefs from around the world! Kat and Andy also share some pretty incredible recipes that they have developed and taste-tested on their own.

Once you get started making your own jerky, the one thing you'll likely learn in a hurry is *I should have made a lot more!*

—Jim Zumbo

# INTRODUCTION

To say that the jerky-world, in just the last five years, has undergone a major renaissance and revival in terms of interests, products, sales, and just plain good eating, would be a huge understatement! Gone are the days of tough, leathery, no-flavor meat, fish, fruit, and veggie offerings. Instead, both commercial producers and homemade/backyard chef offerings of jerky and other dried snacks have elevated themselves to levels of quality, taste, and diversity of product offerings that are truly at a "gourmet" level.

Ten years ago BBQ cook-off competitions were growing in popularity around the nation and television networks/programmers jumped on the BBQing, smoking, and grilling craze with dozens of TV shows and series. It's our guess that it is only a matter

*The RedHead brand dehydrator from Bass Pro Shop is going to make it easy to put up large quantities of dried jerky, snackin' sticks, and other foods all at one time. With the ten metal trays, you've got 2,300 square inches of drying area and a powerful heating element/fan system to make sure the foods dry evenly and quickly.*

of time until these same show producers start up "sponsored jerky" competitions for future TV shows and specials.

*And yes, you can say that you heard it here first!*

On the commercial sales side of jerky/dried snacks, today you'd be hard-pressed to walk into a gas station, convenience store, truck stop, grocery market, and even many of the big-box stores without seeing at least a dozen or more *beefy, meaty, fruity, fishy, or veggie* plastic bag offerings of all kinds and pricey prices!

According to IRI, a Chicago-based marketing/research firm, sales of jerky have soared by 46 percent from 2009 through 2013. Today, that totals over $1.25 billion in sales. Add in sales for the other meat snacks, meat sticks, and ground-protein offerings, and that figure jumps to an astounding $2.3 to $2.5 billion annually.

Once considered a "blue collar" trucker-type grab-and-go snack food, the market is actually catering to more health-conscious shoppers that have discovered that protein is a lot better for their bodies than fats, carbs, and sugars. In addition to being better for your body than a bag of chips or pretzels, the jerky/dried snacks world is now boasting

*Optional Jerky Rack system for the Camp Chef Pellet Grill & Smoker is a great addition to being able to really pile on the meats! Three fine-mesh racks and insert give you nearly 1,600 square inches of inside space for meats and snacks.*

flavor offerings and combinations that many say are "gourmet," while others say that the flavor wars are simply over-the-top.

The downside to the exploding jerky/dried snacks marketplace is twofold. First, when you purchase a commercial product, you never really know what's in it—in terms of where it came from, the quality of raising the animals, and what preservatives are in the bag. Second, if you do a little home arithmetic you'd be shocked at what you are actually paying for these relatively easy and simple-to-make-yourself snacks! The run-of-the-mill/mainstream offerings from all the big-time jerky makers are tagging you $6 to $8 for a 4-ounce package. That's a whopping $24 to $32 a pound!

And for meat, fish, or exotic poultry offerings from a small or localized producer, we've seen $10 pricing for 3-ounce packages. Do the math, and at over $50 a pound, it's no wonder that today's jerky world is a modern day gold rush. As an interesting comparison, commercial jerky that everyone purchases is actually more expensive than live Maine lobster!

If you still question how large the jerky/drying marketplace is, and how it continues to grow, get on your computer and just do an Internet search on jerky, and dried fruits or vegetables. Add a few additional terms such as *recipes, wild game, fish, smoked*, etc., and your total website count is likely to top over *two million listings*. What will then absolutely blow your mind is the fact that many of these individual websites have dozens, if not hundreds, of recipes, tips, spices, marinades, jerky-prep equipment, smokers, dehydrators, pellet/chip stoves, BBQ/grillers, charcoalers, ovens, marinade systems, flavor injectors/enhancers, cutlery, and enough additional accessories to fill an eighteen-wheeler.

Is all that gear, specialized equipment, and gadgetry necessary? The short answer is a simple—no! Do a lot of these products make jerky/dried snacks a lot easier to produce at home? The answer is—yes—and our special thanks to many of our industry friends for sharing some of the latest technology innovations with us so that we can pass along all these new product ideas to our readers. Truly, the product offerings today are far superior to what Grandpa and Grandma had at their disposal, or even what we self-proclaimed Jerky Masters used just a decade ago.

*All Things Jerky* is recipe-ladened and designed for everyone from the supermarket moms who purchase all their meats, fish, poultry, fruits, and vegetables on a weekly basis, to the avid outdoors person that hunts and fishes for most everything found in their freezer. And while protein is a wonderful thing, we've also included a host of easy fruit, vegetable, nut, and snack offerings.

In this book, *All Things Jerky*—we are just that! It is a hard-core compilation of the best tested and submitted recipes from around the world, and all the equipment, gear, and accessories to make it. While the authors are accomplished hunters and anglers, this is not a hunting and fishing how-to book. If you want to know all of that—how to hunt or fish, shot placement, field dressing, and game/fish processing . . . there are dozens of great books to help and teach you.

Instead, having spent the last forty years of sampling jerky/dried snacks from around the world while traveling, hunting, fishing, writing, and doing TV and radio shows, we've amassed recipes that are simple, economical, and easy-to-follow, use easy-to-find ingredients, are fun to make with the entire family, and even better to share with loved ones and friends.

Our book *All Things Jerky* is the definitive guide to making the best jerky and dried snack offerings ever. It is presented with years of field experience, eons of cooking/drying and smoking, decades of trial and error challenges, and a lot of *love*.

We hope you enjoy and share with all.

—Andy Lightbody & Kathy Mattoon

# CHAPTER 1

# JERKY AND THE MEATS—101

Jerky, by the most common definition, is simply using lean meats that have been trimmed of fat, gristle, sinew, and connective tissues, then cut into thin strips and dried to eliminate moisture and prevent spoilage. This is and has been done since ancient times by using salt in the drying process to prevent bacteria from developing/growing on the meats before the moisture has been removed—low-temperature drying or smoking. Jerky meat retains much of the nutritional value of fresh meat but weighs two-thirds to one-half less and takes up a lot less storage space.

Here in the Americas, the modern word for jerky is believed to have been derived from a South American language (Quechua), where the word *ch'arki* means dried and salted meat. Early Spanish/Portuguese explorers supposedly learned from both the native North and South Americans how to process meats, and the word was transformed to the Spanish/Portuguese word of *charque*. And in Asia it's *bakkwa*, *rougan*, or *yuhk gōn*.

As you can see, *All Things Jerky* is an ancient and international love affair!

While all this is interesting and may be useful in your next game of trivia or with your next bar bet, the truth is, dried meats, fruits, and veggies have been around since man crawled out from the darkness of their caves and realized they couldn't eat an entire woolly mammoth, horse, or giant cave bear at once! Drying is simply the world's oldest and most common method of food preservation.

In ancient Egypt, royalty such as the pharaohs were buried with "meat mummies," according to scientists. Dating back to 4000 BC, dried meats and poultry were wrapped in resin-dipped linen.

"The resin flavor would have made it nicer, sort of like teriyaki beef jerky rather than plain beef jerky," said Salima Ikram, Egyptologist at the American University in Cairo, in a 2013 NBC interview. "Tutankhamen had about forty boxes of meat and poultry—remember, he was a growing boy so his appetite was considerable."

Even the United States Department of Agriculture (USDA) point out that drying is not only the oldest way of preserving meats, but canning technology is actually less than two hundred years old. Canning was actually a wartime idea that became a reality with the famous/infamous General Napoleon Bonaparte in Europe during the early 1800s. And as you might guess, freezing wasn't an option until the twentieth century when electricity became available and accessible to homes and food producers.

Most meats and fish contain about 60 to 70 percent water. Fruits and veggies contain 80 to 90 percent. When the foods are dried, that water content is reduced to 3 to 10 percent, and both the weight and volume of the foods are shrunk to one-half to one-quarter of what they were originally.

Today, modern jerkies (commercial and homemade)—muscle meats, ground meat snacks, fruits, and veggies—are normally brined, marinated, or dry-spice rubbed and dehydrated, dried, or smoked with low heat (135–200°F). Fruits and veggies are best smoked/dried at the lower temperatures, while all the meats need to be in the 160–200°F range. Equipment options run from home ovens, dryers, and dehydrators, to smokers, BBQs, charcoalers, and grillers.

All you have to do is look at all the options. Every sportsman's mail-order catalog or website has upward of ten or fifteen catalog pages featuring dozens of smokers, dehydrators, spices, jerky guns, meat grinders, slicers, cutlery, smoking woods, vacuum packers, and accessories for homemade jerky products.

## MEET THE MEATS

Virtually any type of edible meat (domestic or wild), poultry, fowl, small game, or fish can be made into jerky, and the vast majority of it—even some of the off-the-wall varieties—taste pretty darn good! While beef is certainly #1 for non-hunters, bison, goat, sheep/lamb, yak, and pork are also favorites in the domestic meats department. In the wild game department, the overall favorites are venison (deer), elk, antelope, caribou, moose, bear, wild hog, exotics, waterfowl, turkey, upland birds, gator, and some small game. Snake, mountain lion, bobcat, coon, opossum, coyote, muskrat, beaver, lynx, marmot, emu/ostrich, and bugs/worms are edible and "jerkable," but really fall more into the novelty category instead of mainstream choices.

Bottom line is, when it comes to jerky, virtually everything you can clean, carve, slice, season, and dry . . . can make some great jerky.

Far and away, the most popular choices for making great jerky at home are roasts, steaks, chops, or most any of the animal's "muscle meat."

Setting the record straight, once and for all . . . domestic beef (even free range) and others (sheep, goat, pigs, turkey, and chicken) are not going to have the same taste as wild game animals. Cows don't

*Jerky medallions.*
*Photo courtesy of Traeger Wood Pellet Grills.*

move around much and live on a diet of wild grass, hay, etc. Game animals (big, small, birds) by comparison have a much more diverse diet, have to work for their food by moving or migrating, and are always on the alert for predators. Wild game simply has a different taste than domestics.

Beef to an urbanite/non-hunter has great flavor, and there is nothing wrong with it. After all, according to the USDA, the average American consumes over 275 pounds of it each year. Beef to an avid outdoorsman/hunter is kind of bland. The beauty of beef and other domestic game is that it is readily available year-round, can be purchased at every grocery store, with various cuts that are ideal for making great jerky with all your favorite recipes here. Although any of the meats purchased at the store are not *cheap*, by watching the grocery ads, you can often find discounted prices in your newspaper.

Domestic meats from the butcher or the grocery store are ready to jerky process as soon as you get them home. However, when it comes to wild game (big and small), the Oregon State University Extension Service says game meats should be frozen for at least sixty days at 0°F to kill parasites.

While the "fat" on a cow, sheep, or hog is often a good thing and a source of additional flavor/tenderness when baking, broiling, and BBQing, it is for the most part not a real good thing for making jerky at home. The same is true with any wild game—big, small, poultry, or waterfowl. Fat does not dry, dehydrate or add anything to dried/smoked meats. In fact it makes the meat greasy, greasy tasting, and accelerates your jerky becoming rancid, moldy, and inedible.

So whether you are using beef, other domestic meats, or any type of wild game—trim off all the fat that you can! In addition, trim off any gristle, membranes, and connective tissue that can make your jerky tough. A wise old man (Andy's dad) taught him a long time ago that "when you trim it completely and trim it right, you don't need strong teeth to chew it all night."

## MUSCLE MEATS

So what are the best cuts of muscle meat? There are several top choices, but the general rule of thumb is that the meat is lean and contains little fat or marbling. Keep in mind, even tougher cuts of meat will tenderize a lot once you brine or marinade them. If your cuts are really tough, you might want to dig out the old meat hammer/pounder or needle tenderizer that is likely hidden away in your kitchen, and do a little "at-home tenderizing" before you brine or marinate. And when it comes to slicing the meat into strips, cut with the grain for a chewier jerky and against the grain for an easier and more tooth-friendly feast. Regardless of the cuts, jerky strips absorb maximum flavors from the dry rubs or wet marinades when they are cut into strips that are around ¼-inch in thickness. Go ½-inch or thicker, and any flavor additions to your meat will be slow to nonexistent in

*Often called a "buffalo," it's actually the American bison and has been a great-eating staple for thousands of years. Roasts, steaks, and ground bison meat is readily available at many grocery stores today and makes delicious and lean jerky or snackin' sticks. Photo courtesy of USDA.*

penetrating the meat all the way through. (See Chapter 7, about spices, rubs, marinades, and woods).

"As a general rule, any/all marinades will take about twenty-four hours or longer to break down the muscle meats strips, tenderize them to the max, and allow them to absorb all the flavors of your dry rubs or even wet marinades," says Hans Hummel, jerky king and president of Hi Mountain Seasonings (www.himtnjerky.com). "Unless you have a powerful vacuum/flavor infusion system, you just can't really rush this part of the process in making jerky."

***Flank Steak:*** By far, this is the jerky maker's favorite cut! It is often called a London Broil and is really the belly muscle of the animal. It's rather slim/thin and has the shape of a slab of bacon. It is very lean and cuts easily into jerky strips—either with the grain of the meat or across the grain.

***Top/Bottom Round:*** Both come from the hindquarter/leg of the animal. Major meat sections are loaded with lean meat that is ideal for roasts or round steaks that can be cut into long jerky strips—either with or against the grain. Bottom Round cuts have more connective tissues and require more trimming, and may be a candidate for some home-grown tenderizing.

***Eye of Round:*** This is the smallest cut of muscle meat out of the hindquarter. It is rated as relatively tough, but still rates high as a favorite for making into jerky strips. On the plus side, it is often offered on sale at lower prices than other cuts. Tenderizing is always an option.

***Sirloin Tip:*** This cut also comes from the hindquarter and is also called a Round Tip Steak, Tip Steak, Silver Tip, Sandwich Steak, Ball Tip Steak, Breakfast Steak, and even a Knuckle Steak. However, don't be fooled by *Sirloin* being included in the name. It is not a *Top Sirloin*. It is however both a lean and excellent cut of meat for making jerky.

***Chuck:*** Chuck steaks and roasts come from the front quarter as compared to an animal's hindquarter or hip. The *Chuck* cuts are in and around the neck area, and go back toward the ribs. Cuts from this area have a lot of flavor, but are often marbled and fatty. It can be used for jerky, but plan on a lot of trimming.

***Skirt Steak:*** The *Skirt* is a thin, fibrous muscle that is actually the animal's diaphragm muscle, which separates the abdomen from the chest. At the grocery store, it's a cut of meat that is often packaged for making fajitas. It's a rather chewy piece of meat, but trims

*Just about all cuts of game meat can be transformed into delicious jerky strips. We use the White River Sendero Bush knife, which was designed by noted knife maker Jerry Fisk to handle the tough chunking and trimming.*

*Out of the box and ready for you to mix, Hi Mountain Seasonings are some of the best eighteen blends and cures that you will find on the marketplace today. As premixed products they are pretty good. Our recipes, and add-on spices to theirs, are even better!*

well and strips into nice jerky strips either with the grain or across it. It's also an ideal candidate for a needle or hammer tenderizer.

**Brisket:** The *Brisket* is the front portion of the beef breast and is found between the front legs. It too is fibrous and fatty. It's not a top choice for making jerky because of the high fat/marbling.

## GROUND MEAT

For the most part, this kind of jerky strip or stick is simply called a "meat snack." Non-muscle meat jerky strips that are made up of "ground/processed" meat snacks account for nearly $1.5 billion a year in sales at grocery stores, gas stations, liquor stores, and convenience stores. Why? Because these processed meat sticks, rolls, and strips often have a softer and easier *chew factor*, with many of the same great flavors as muscle meat jerky.

If you're a hunter and process your big game meats, you know that there are always a lot of trimmings—meat and fat—that can't be sliced and stripped into jerky slices.

*The Weston Supply meat grinders come with three stainless steel grinding plates for fine, medium, and coarse grinds. The medium grind (left) is the one that will work best when making our snackin' sticks.*

If you process your meat and then make some into ground meat, this is a great way to avoid having to make pounds and pounds of hamburger and being able to kick it to a level that rivals anything you can purchase over the counter. Like making homemade jerky: why spend upward of $40 a pound for commercial offerings when you can make your own for less than $8 a pound?

If you are going to home-process the game trimmings, we suggest that you actually add about a third to half of some more prime cuts and good jerky meat to your grinding process. This makes it much leaner, less fatty, and makes the drying/smoking process go faster.

If you are not grinding and processing your own meat and want to make some of the best meat snack sticks, ask the butcher in charge of your meat department at the grocery store to find/select a couple of steaks or roasts that are on sale that week to grind them to a *medium-grind consistency.* Most stores will do this for customers at no charge. Make sure that the meat is ground to a medium consistency—not fine or coarse. Coarse grind is great for making homemade chili, but not ideal for jerky snacks. Fine grinding is close to "mush" level, and we've never found a practical use for it.

If your butcher does the grind for you (and we suggest looking for what is on sale, and whether it's a lean cut or fatty), don't add any additional fat or suet (beef fat) to it. Remember, just like muscle meat jerky, leaner is better and best for the jerky-meat snacks. If you have to buy prepackaged burger/grind meat, go for those that are 10–15 percent fat added or less. Those that have higher fat levels (20–25 percent) are simply not ideal for jerky snack meat making.

## PORK/BACON

Both domestic pork and wild hogs are ideal for making homemade jerky, as well as bacon! We'll say it here, and again repeat ourselves when we get into the recipes, but there is controversy about using using/preparing pork for making jerky—cooked or uncooked. The controversy is over whether it is better to pre-cook pork to 160°F before making it into jerky or use the raw pork and make sure it reaches an internal temperature of 160°F as it is turned into jerky or meat snacks. Information on both sides of the "pork debate" can be

*Kathy Mattoon took this good-eating size Texas wild hog with a .25 caliber Benjamin pellet rifle. A head shot at twenty-two yards, and the hunt was over.*

found through the National Center for Home Processing and Preservation (headquartered at the University of Georgia and Alabama A&M University) at www.nchfp.uga.edu.

As with any big game headed for the jerky dryers/smokers, we suggest that the fresh meat cuts be stored in your freezer for a minimum of sixty days at 0°F to ensure that any bacteria, disease, or pathogens are killed and safe to final process. On the flip side, the National Center says in its reports, "If you choose to heat the meat prior to drying to decrease the risk of foodborne illness, do so at the end of the marination time. To heat, bring strips and marinade to a boil and boil for five minutes before draining and drying. If strips are more than ¼ inch thick, the length of time may need to be increased. If possible, check the temperature of several strips with a metal stem-type thermometer to determine that 160°F has been reached."

This might work well if you are using those recipes with a wet marinade, but it simply does not work well if you are using a dry rub. Here is where you will need to follow the instructions above, but boil your meat strips, pat dry, and then add your dry rub flavorings and salt mix. Then begin your marinating process for around twenty-four hours to ensure best flavor.

As a suggested alternative, you can (if you want to) place raw pork strips in your home oven that is set to 160°F. Place your jerky in the oven for about 30–45 minutes as an added precaution against trichinella (pork worm), *E. coli,* or salmonella. Once again, it comes down to personal choices and options. We just wanted to present you with both options.

Do keep in mind that all pork is likely to have considerably more fat than other meats, so plan on trimming off all you can. Front shoulders, often called pork butts, are usually fatter than the hindquarter cuts or the hams.

If you are planning on making bacon jerky, you can use either commercially prepackaged/smoked bacon from the market, or if you are more ambitious . . . you can actually smoke and make your own by using a fresh pork belly. And yes, the pork belly is exactly what it sounds like—the meat and fat from the underside of the hog. It becomes bacon once you have brined it, smoked it, and sliced it. Whether you use your own or store-bought bacon, make sure that the bacon is sliced "thin." The "thick cut" bacon should be reserved for breakfast and BLTs.

And while we all know that thanks to bacon, the world is a much better place in which to live, keep in mind that bacon jerky does not have the same low-fat meat profile of wild game or even beef. A 1-ounce serving of big game jerky can have less than 1 gram of fat, whereas beef is between 1–2 grams. An equal serving of bacon jerky has between 8–9 grams.

## POULTRY AND WATERFOWL

Chicken, turkey (domestic/wild), waterfowl, and upland birds all can be made into some of the best-tasting jerky you can imagine. It also generates controversy about using the meats raw or precooked. Like pork, it can be sliced into strips and boiled for about five minutes, or semi-baked in your home oven for about thirty minutes at 160°F.

*Filleting out a limit of dove is well worth the effort. The meat carves easily away from the breastbone and the dark meat is rich and flavorful when marinated and smoked into jerky chunks.*

And while some "meat purists" are going to holler—*foul!* We simply *breast out* everything from dove to snow geese and pheasants to big tom turkeys. Messing with the legs and thighs really doesn't produce enough meat to warrant all the extra work, especially when you have a giant pile of birds waiting to be cleaned.

If you are buying from the grocery store, chicken breasts and thighs are an easy and tasty alternative for any wild game birds. Make sure that you debone breasts and thighs, and remove the skin.

## FISH

Scientists say that there are over twenty thousand species of combined fresh and saltwater fish on planet earth, and most all are edible. Add in other treats such as lobster and shrimp, and it's no wonder that smoked and dried/jerky offerings are growing in popularity. Dehydrating/drying—with or without smoking—can really bring out some unique flavors, without making it fishy tasting. Lean fish or those with a fat content of less than 5 percent are the top choices for jerking. Some of these species include bass, panfish, walleye, pike, cod, halibut, cod, croaker, flounder, haddock, monkfish, pollock, rockfish, sea bass, snapper, sea trout, and sole.

Fish with a higher fat content can also be used for jerky, but require a little more attention when drying, and should not be kept at room temperature for more than a few days. Refrigerating can extend the shelf life for several weeks, and freezing will keep it all for months. Some of those fattier species include trout, salmon, catfish, carp, tuna, mackerel, shark, bonito, mullet, Pacific yellowtail, and tuna.

Fresh fish are always the best, but if they have been well cared for before freezing, you'll find you can still make some neat treats. Fresh fish, if you have not personally caught and cared for them, should never ever smell "fishy." They should have bright/shiny eyes and red/pink gills with an overall "fresh appearance," and not like something that was dragged around up and down boat docks! Any whole frozen fish you may purchase should be defrosted slowly in the refrigerator, and filleted and brined as soon as it is partially thawed.

Cooked fish can also be dried and smoked, and in some areas of the world it is considered a delicacy and better than fresh fish. However, it has a different taste than true fish jerky.

# CHAPTER 2

# BASICS TO JERKY AND SNACK DRYING— HOME OVENS AND DEHYDRATORS

In the world of preserving virtually all foods, there are basically four ways of processing for preserving. You can cook them, freeze them, dry them, or pickle them. Probably the easiest of the three methods is cooking the food, which has been the standard since ancient times. The downside of that is you have to eat what you cook, and it's tough preserving the leftovers for any extended periods of time.

Pickling certainly extends the shelf life of meats, veggies, and fruits, but requires a lot of preparation and specialized equipment and takes up a tremendous amount of shelf and storage space.

Drying by comparison is relatively easy, more affordable, and requires a lot less specialized equipment. The dry foods have a long storage life and are both lighter in weight and take up a lot less storage room!

The most basic and long-standing method of drying any/all foods is air and sunshine. Ancients simply gathered whatever they harvested, hunted, or fished and prepared it for Mother Nature to take over. It certainly worked, but by today's standards it's not really efficient, flavorful, or in many cases even safe to consume. Filling your backyard with solar drying stations is likely not to impress your neighbors. Dozens of food-drying racks laid out individually for maximum sun-gathering and air circulation is rather cumbersome by comparison to six-tray smokers and twelve-tray dehydrators that take up relatively little indoor or backyard space. Add to the fact that using this ancient/cowboy method is not very productive in high humidity areas. When it rains or snows or if it's just been cloudy for a few days, temperatures can be near or below freezing. All that said, you can see why this method rates as being more of a novelty and a way to earn a merit badge, or as a last resort for survivalists and preppers.

A more practical method involves utilizing the world of *technology*, one that is readily available for all styles of making dried meats, vegetables, and fruits! Gone are the days where drying and smoking something required a culinary degree or a lot of extreme time or attention. Home ovens, dehydrators, smokers, grillers, and BBQs have made home prep easier than it was ten or even five years ago, as each year the major manufacturers continue to introduce evolutionary and sometimes revolutionary new offerings.

In the jerky/snack making accessory world, our basic opinion is: if you can't find it today, you likely don't need it. However, you can likely expect someone is going to come along and invent it soon!

For the home drier/smoker fan, the accessory product world has totally exploded. Many are great ideas, while others are just gadgets that will end up in the kitchen draw and gather dust. A quick Internet search will leave your head swimming with well over two million listings/offerings of cutlery, sharpeners, meat cutters/slices, wood flavors (chips, chunks and pellets), meat grinders, jerky shooters/guns, vacuum sealers, gloves, aprons, cold smokers, brines, rubs, and marinades.

# HOME OVENS

Today, with the modern convenience of gas or electric ovens in everyone's home kitchen, jerky makers on a budget or wanting to stay with the "absolute basics" have one of the finest jerky maker/dryers to ever come along. And, if your oven has a "convection/ air fan" feature, it is not only easy to keep your temperatures low for drying, but circulate air around your foods to even better dry.

*Hi Mountain Seasonings makes a host of jerky-making accessories, including jerky guns and metal small-mesh racks. Their racks are great for using in your home oven because of their small and convenient size.*

Home ovens for drying simply need to be set for low temperatures (160–200°F) before you place your oven racks of foods inside. Simply keep the food slices/jerky about a ½-inch apart for optimum drying and air circulation. Keep in mind that, when drying, you are not trying to *cook* your foods. Instead you want them to simply *dry*, lose 90 to 95 percent of the raw moisture value, and turn themselves into dried, crispy snacks.

A few of the downside features of using your home oven for doing a lot of drying of meats, fruits, and veggies is that most home ovens, while having 5.8 to 6.9 cubic feet of capacity, only come with 1–3 oven racks. Even though they have slide-in spacer areas for up to 5–7 racks, the oven/stove manufacturers usually only include 2–3 racks as standard equipment. Their reasoning is that you are going to be using the oven for cooking in various pan sizes, with various food heights (flat pizza to a tall turkey) and

*The problem with most racks from the home oven is that they have large gaps and spacing that can cause your meats and eats to fall through the cracks! Metal racks with small mesh designs, as well as plastic/Teflon racks are available as accessory items. Be careful using plastic wraps in your oven or smoker. Many are not rated to above 175°F, and they will melt!*

need the convenience of being able to adjust the racks, or eliminate them when cooking foods with a large overhead clearance.

Finding additional racks to be able to do a full drying load of foods is often a crapshoot, as the actual internal dimensions of your oven and the racks can vary by the manufacturer. And if you are lucky enough to find them through the oven manufacturer, they are expensive! Ranging from $40–$70 each and rarely including the shipping costs, for what 3–5 additional oven racks are going to cost, you can purchase a variety of pretty nice smokers or dehydrators. However, as an entry-level dryer who may not be planning on making many racks of dried snacks at one time, the home oven is a great way to get acquainted with *All Things Jerky*.

Another disadvantage to the home oven racks is that the wire racks have large open holes or slits, where it can make laying out your jerky for drying a lot more challenging. Trying to get fruits, veggies, and meat strips to balance on the wire can be frustrating. For drying meats that have been cut into long (6–8 inch) strips, they can be draped over the wire racking and pinned with toothpicks. The only other alternative to wire rack "wide spaces and gaps" syndrome is to purchase a few of the may aftermarket drying racks (metal or plastic) and placing them on top of your existing oven racks. They are usually sized like a smaller mesh pattern and are a great way to keep your foods from falling through the cracks.

Metal wire racks such as those offered by Hi Mountain Seasonings (www.himtnjerky.com) and Weston (www.westonsupply.com ) are small and inexpensive accessory racks that have a ¼-inch crosshatch pattern that allows you to lay your foods out evenly spaced for drying. Some jerky accessory makers offer nonstick Teflon coated racks, but they are pricier than the chromed metal ones. A quick squirt on any oven drying rack with a commercial no-stick spray, or a gentle wipe with a paper towel and vegetable oil, will work equally well.

Some accessory makers also offer lightweight plastic screens that are preformed or can be cut from a roll like plastic wrap/aluminum foil. Unless your oven is really, really calibrated to not go to above 200°F, it's suggested that these be avoided. They often melt, make a big molten plastic mess in your oven, and can ruin your dried foods.

## DEHYDRATORS

A dehydrator in the simplest terms is a *fancy electric food drying machine.* While they don't impart any smoke or cook flavoring into the meats or veggies, they can be used in your indoor kitchen, garage, camper/trailer, etc., without setting off the smoke alarms.

They run from basic and relatively inexpensive temperature controlled models, all the way to fancy and more pricey versions with timers, automatic shutoffs, digital controls, and LED displays. All of them remove the moisture from your foods and help to preserve it by drying it out. Dehydrators use a heat source, and most often a fan or airflow circulation system that further reduces the

*Home dehydrators are ideal for putting up jerky, snackin' sticks, and lots of fruits, veggies, and other treats. A few manufacturers not only have a wide variety of home models, but also make giant commercial dryers as well. The 2 Zone NSF Commercial Dehydrator from Excalibur is designed for the pro that is planning on going into the business of dried foods.*

water content of fruits, veggies, and meats. Dehydrators are extremely economical to use and according to jerky makers, they average 2–4 cents an hour to operate.

Be warned that there are still "cheapy" dehydrators being sold today that have only an on/off heating element switch and no air circulation fans. Avoid these like the *plague,* as there is no way to monitor the exact drying temperatures, and with no fan, there is little direct moving air around the food items! To ensure even and uniform drying, you have to rotate the trays from top to bottom on a regular basis, which means you have to practically stand over your dehydrator for the duration of the drying process.

Another feature or concern worth noting is whether you should choose a plastic dehydrator or one made of metal. Not that the plastic models are inefficient, but there is a controversy about chemical/plastic safety and a chemical called BPA (bisphenol A). While the U.S. Environmental Protection Agency (EPA) says that plastics with this chemical have low amounts that pose no human health risks, others say the chemical actually migrates out of the plastic and into the food, and can cause damage to the brain, and health effects to infants and children.

Some dehydrator manufacturers are now actually certifying and marking their products as "BPA free." Others have changed the plastic formula in the drying screens/trays to eliminate BPA, and say that while the plastic shells/exterior are not BPA free, with the food never touching those parts, any concerns are unwarranted.

Excalibur Dehydrators (www.excaliburdehydrator.com) say on their website, "The screens are BPA free; the rest of the unit is not. The screen is what the food sits on to dehydrate. So food is *not* in contact with polycarbonate, therefore migration of BPA is virtually impossible. Studies show that there is less than .005 milligrams per kilo of food/beverage of BPA that migrates from polycarbonate when in contact. This is very low and below the safety standards set by US government agencies. At this typical level of migration, an average person that weighs 132 lbs would have to ingest more than 600 kilos of food or

*Making your own different types of fruit rollups is going to save you lots of money at the grocery store! A blender, some applesauce, and a few spices, and you are ready to make your own affordable treats in the Nesco dehydrator. Raspberry (top left) can be finished off with powdered sugar for a little extra sweetness. Jelly and peanut butter are going to be an the iconic favorite, especially for the kids (top right). And the banana rollup with nuts (bottom) is an adult favorite.*

beverage in contact with polycarbonate every day for an entire lifetime to exceed the safe intake."

A few of our favorite dehydrators come from Nesco, Weston Products, and the Bass Pro Shop's RedHead brand. While there are literally dozens of dehydrator companies, and forty or more models to select from, spend a little research time and figure out what is best for your needs and your budget. One of the best overall features with the electric dehydrators is the low cost of operation. Stats show that the average cost is between 2–4 cents/hour. That's a bargain every cost-conscious jerky/snack maker can relate to!

The large stainless steel model with ten removable trays from RedHead (www.basspro.com) features a powerful air circulation fan, a fifteen-hour digital timer, 95–155°F temperature control, and a cavernous 2,300 square inches of drying capacity/space. It also has a unique feature in that the drying chamber itself can be detached from the unit without having to remove the individual drying trays. This makes it much more convenient if you need to carry the drying racks, loaded up with foods, from one location to another before unloading!

Nesco (www.nesco.com), also known as American Harvest brand, has a huge line of dehydrators that range from small to humongous! At the top of the line is a rectangular plastic FD-2000 with six stackable trays and mesh screens. It puts out 530 watts of power to the heating element and the air circ fan. While not the most powerful (by wattage) in our experience, the unit has a sealed/gasket-type lid that does a great job of holding the selected temperatures steady and circulating the air efficiently. The unit has large digital LED displays/dials and an automatic timer for up to twenty-four hours of drying time, and it is adjustable from 95–160°F.

*Nesco has a full line of quality and affordable dehydrators for drying meats, fruits, vegetables, rollups, and much more. Use a nonstick spray on your dryer trays to keep everything from sticking and grabbing.*

Weston Supply (www.westonsupply.com) has both plastic and stainless steel dehydrator offerings. The biggest is their stainless steel, 2,160-square-inch (15-square-foot) model with ten large, removable chrome-plated trays. It is rated to 1,000 watts of power and has a horizontal air circ system with lots of vents. The fan in their dehydrator is so quiet that we literally

*Remember . . . where's there's smoke, there's flavor! The Smoke Chief cold smoke unit produces billowing clouds of smoke that can be run through your charcoaler or propane BBQ and grill. With a little heat from the grill and a lot of smoke, you can tailor your jerky flavors to a variety of wood pellets.*

had to open the door and peak inside to make sure it was running! It has a twelve-hour timer, an automatic shutoff feature, and a color-coded thermostat that is adjustable from 84–155°F.

With the food slices/meat strips on the plastic or metal racks/trays, the dehydrator temperature is then set to coincide with the drying process, depending on what kind of foods you are processing. The overall process is pretty simple, and it is the dehydrator's heating element that warms the food and causes the moisture to be released. The dryer's fan then blows out the warm/moist air from the interior, via air vents. If the dehydrator has an automatic timer system, the unit is set for the manufacturer's suggested drying times (hours) until the food is dried and the moisture is reduced. Meats are usually reduced by 90 to 95 percent of their original moisture, while fruits and veggies are down by 75 to 80 percent of their raw state.

Constant controlled heat and air circulation are the key to successful dehydration and drying. It's not rocket science, but room/outside air temperatures and ambient humidity levels can factor into and change the total drying times. We suggest you the maker's guidelines and charts as a general rule and adjust your drying times accordingly.

Most meats are dehydrated at a higher temperature of from 155–165°F, because of the concerns about bacteria/pathogens. You may even want to preheat your dehydrator to that level before putting your meats in. Vegetables and fruits seem to do best at the 135–145°F settings. And if you are doing nuts, temperatures should be further reduced to between 90–125°F. Many nuts have natural oils in them and, when heated to 135°F or higher, actually seem to "cook," and can be left with a strong or rancid taste.

Remember, once any foods are dried and removed from the dehydrator, they need to be sealed and stored in some sort of airtight containers. A lot of foods will actually pick up humidity and moisture by being left out in the air and not sealed. Vacuum sealed bags, airtight plastic containers, or even glass canning jars are a top choice for keeping your dried foods/snacks dry!

## CHAPTER 3

# IF YOU GOT 'EM ... SMOKE 'EM!

## WHAT IS A SMOKER?

The modern world of commercially-made smokers for home jerky/dried food making has exploded with new technologies over the last few years, and that has taken out a great deal of the time, trouble, and *mystery* about of being able to produce great tasting smoky snacks. Like dehydrators/dryers, these smokers and grills, when used to make jerky, fruits, and veggies, are not supposed to "cook" the food. Instead, they "dry" the food at relatively low temperature and give the home chef the opportunity to impart various wood flavors into the foods by smoldering/burning charcoal, wood chips, chunks, pellets, pellet briquettes, or wood bisquettes.

Charcoal/hardwood BBQs and grills were once the mainstay for early jerky makers, simply because that is what was readily available and affordable. Today, if you want to start a fight about as passionate as a discussion about religion, politics, or whether the Chicago Cubs will ever win a World Series, just bring up the subject of liquid propane (LP)/electric versus charcoal/hardwood smokers. Both sides of the "smoke wars" have their strong points, and it often comes down to personal choices. According to the 2013 statistics from the Hearth, Patio and Barbecue Association (HPBA), most Americans prefer and are purchasing gas/propane BBQ grills and smokers. A total of 58 percent are LP burner buddies, as compared to 40 percent that are identified as charcoal cookers. Only 2 percent say that they like to plug-and-cook/smoke with electricity.

Some of the obvious reasons that propane is more popular than charcoal for making jerky and snacks include convenience, faster setup time, less mess, easier cleanup, and better regulation of drying temperatures and the amount of smoke on/into the foods.

## ELECTRIC SMOKERS

If you are into statistics, electric smokers account for less than three hundred thousand of the nearly fourteen million smokers/grillers that are sold annually. It seems that propane smokers are simply the king-of-the hill product.

Of all the many electric models that are available today, probably the most iconic and readily recognizable of the long-time electric home smokers is the Little Chief, which was introduced back in 1968 and continues to be popular today. Made by Smokehouse Products (www.smokehouseproducts.com) in Oregon, it is a simple, no-frills, direct-heat/smoke aluminum shell-type smoker. It has a non-temperature regulated electric heating element (up to 165°F), several metal racks, and a removable front panel to allow access to the food loading area. Since its introduction almost fifty years ago, little has changed other than the addition of larger and smaller models. Smoke is made from a heating element at the bottom of the unit where a small pan of various types of wood chips can be placed to gently smoke and heat the interior. All Little Chief, Big Chief, and Mini Chief models are relatively inexpensive, and are great entry-level smokers for the beginner. They come with easy-to-follow plug-and-smoke directions that turn out some great smoked foods for those wanting to make smaller batches of jerky and other eats.

Smokers in this class are fueled and flavored by using wood chips, chunks, or pellets. With the chip and chunk smokers, you have to manually charge or place the wood in the fire/wood pans and you have to remember to recharge or refill it after about an hour for additional smoke. Many are direct heat/smoke, meaning that the heating element and wood fire pan are directly below the jerky with little or no heat barrier.

*Newest innovation for the jerk master who has and wants everything is the Masterbuilt electric smoker, which now comes with a Bluetooth remote control system! Most major functions are now internally monitored, sent wirelessly to the remote control.*

Moving up in cost and with more features are a covey of other electric smokers and makers. While we are all about making jerky/snacks with all our smokers, keep in mind that, like us, you'll likely end up doing a lot more traditional meat smoking and cooking with whatever brand you purchase. Here is where it is important to check out a variety of makes, models, temperature ranges, sizes, and price offerings.

All electric smokers have a heating element, much like you have in an electric oven. A lot of their popularity for use in making jerky and snacks is because many of them have temperature controls adjustable from 125–250°F. That's a *plus* for making jerky and snacks where you want the 130–225°F temps and good smoke.

On the downside, many have a maximum temperature of 250°F and leave you no other options if you want higher temperature settings. Only a few are rated to 400°F.

A few electric smokers you may want to consider with good to great testing and consumer ratings come from:

*The Masterbuilt Company* (www.masterbuilt.com) offers both analog and digital electric smokers. Some even come with remote timer and temperature controls. Smokers have dual-wall construction. The newest innovation for the ultimate couch potato BBQer/jerker is their new Bluetooth digital model. With your handheld device, you can control and monitor virtually all functions of the smoker, including on/off, cooking temperature/time, internal light, and meat temperature. Unfortunately, you still have to get your tail off the couch to reload the smoking pan with wood chunks. *Sorry about that!*

*Smokin Tex* (www.smokintex.com) has a large line of electric smokers designed for the backyard jerker, all the way up to expensive professional models. All units have fully-insulated walls for maintaining consistent heat control, and a cool outside shell temperature. Optional wheels are a plus for moving the smoker around easily. Theirs use chips, chunks, or pellets and have temperature thermostat controls. Two unique accessories also available are their *Jerky Dryer* and their *Pro Series Cold Smoke* plate.

Their *Jerky Dryer* is a small metal canister that simply sits atop the unit's top air/smoke vent. It has a twelve-volt electric fan (power supply included/no special wiring) that draws the air from the smoker's interior and through the jerky. The *Pro Series Cold Smoke* plate (available in several sizes) is an insulated plate that serves as a heat blocker when you want the smoke without the heat. It slides in over the heating element/smoke box and is used in conjunction with a drip pan full of ice cubes! It's an innovative solution for making homemade smoked cheeses, salts, paprika, and more.

*Outdoor Leisure Products* (www.olp-inc.com) electric smoker with the *Smoke Hollow* brand name is an inexpensive but reliable entry-level unit for the novice. It stands thirty inches in height, has a simple plug-in temperature regulator, and a door-mounted thermometer gauge. Nothing fancy, no frills, but a unit worth looking at if you are just getting started.

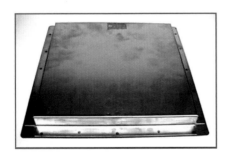
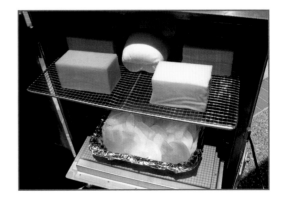

*The cold smoke plate from Smokin Tex is an insulated plate that you use in your smoker by putting a pan of ice cubes on top. It allows you to cold-smoke cheeses and other foods, and keeps the heat down by allowing the ice to slowly melt.*

*Bradley Smoker's* (www. bradleysmoker.com) entire line of smokers are electric and rather unique in that they will *only* use small *Bradley bisquettes* (wood pucks) as the smoking source. They will not work with chips, chunks, or wood pellets. On the plus side, they have a large selection of wood flavors to choose from. Analog and digital models are available and are temperature-controlled to smoke to around 250–280°F in a variety of sizes.

Newly introduced from Bradley is a two-rack compact smoker. Temperature, time, and smoke digital controls are up to 350°F,

*Bradley electric smokers are mostly large-capacity units that are designed to use their wood puck or bisquettes in a variety of flavors. Temperature controls for smoking are up to 250°F, with a max temp of 320°F.*

and it has a convection fan to circulate air around foods. Like all their smokers, the wood puck feeding tube can be loaded up with their briquettes and left unattended for hours. Their owner's manual says the smoker is for household use only, and must be protected from the weather if used outside. The unit comes with a smoke exhaust hose for connecting to a vented exhaust hood or placed outside a window. From what we've heard, the unit would seem to work best when used outside or in a well-ventilated area or shed.

## ELECTRIC SMOKER/GRILL COMBOS

While generally more expensive than a simple home-type electric smoker, the versatility of having both a smoker and a grill-type barbeque combination is undeniable! Instead of having to purchase two appliances, the electric combo smoker and griller lets the home chef set up the unit for everything from low to high temperatures and select the amount of smoke to be used on the foods. These have automatic thermostats, meat probes, and large-capacity wood pellet reservoirs.

*Traeger Wood Pellet Grills* (www.traegergrills.com) has been making electric smokers/ grillers since the 1990s and offers a full line for everyone from the backyard smoker and BBQer/jerker to the professional. They are big, heavy-duty smokers that will not only likely last you a lifetime, but will be something that you'll pass on to your children!

Traeger's Texas model is designed to look like the old-fashioned Texas-style wood cookers, but with a twenty-first century twist. Today, it features a high-tech wood pellet

*The small two-rack electric smoker from Bradley is designed for smoking and drying small amounts of food. It works like their larger smokers and can use only their bisquettes. It is supposed to be for indoor use with a flexible hose to vent it outside, but many feel it's better used in an outdoor kitchen or well-ventilated area.*

system that takes a lot of the time and trouble out of jerky and snack smoking. The Texas Elite model (one of about twenty in their lineup) tips the scales at 140 pounds and has an automatic wood pellet auger that feeds a 36,000 BTU burner. It also has an electronic auto start system and a multi-position digital thermometer control.

The smoker/grill is fully adjustable from 180–375°F, and it features a full 646-square-inch internal grill area that can be greatly expanded by adding their optional jerky/snack drying rack. One unique option/accessory for some of the Traeger smokers/grills is their *Cold Smoke* box that easily bolts onto various models. In addition to being able to cook of a big load of jerky on the heated side, the Cold Smoke box is a great way to add your favorite wood smoke flavor to cheeses, smoked salts, thin-sliced fish, and a host of fruits and vegetables without adding much heat.

*Camp Chef Products* (www.campchef.com), longtime maker of propane smokers, grilles, stoves, ovens, and just about everything you need to cook out of doors, has recently launched a new line of electric smokers/grillers with all the features for doing everything from BBQing to jerky and snack making. Quality of their products is unsurpassed, and they are priced affordably, even as compared to many competitors. Three smoker/grill models are currently offered and range in size with an internal food-capacity of from 429 to 560 square inches of rack surface area.

That's a lot of cooking/smoking area for BBQing and a moderate amount of space for drying jerky and snacks. Camp Chef has increased the drying/smoking space with an optional/unique *Jerky Rack insert*. The frame and the racks easily slip in and fit inside the smoke/cooking chamber, nearly quadrupling the smoking area up to a whopping 1,584 square inches! The three metal racks have a smaller mesh pattern, as compared to regular smoker racks, and are ideal for smaller items like fruits, veggies, and jerky strips.

*The Traeger Tex Wood Pellet Grille comes with an optional cold smoke box that bolts onto the unit. It's a great addition for smoked cheese, fruits, vegetables, salts, and anything you want to smoke, but you will need to keep the heat temperatures low.*

*At the heart of the wood pellet smokers, grills, and stoves is the auger that moves the flavored wood pellets from the reservoir to the burner. Many like the Camp Chef model are adjustable for more or less smoke and pellets depending upon what you are drying and smoking.*

The pellet hopper capacity is 18–20 pounds of your favorite flavored wood pellets, so there are no worries about running out of smoke for your foods. Smoke infusion is regulated by an electronic auto-start ignition system, and you can easily adjust the amount of smoke (low or high). On the low-smoke setting, it will produce great smoke and keep the internal temperature to around 160°F. On the high-smoke setting, it raises the temperature to 220°F. Or if you want to adjust everything on your own for the BBQing options, the unit is fully-adjustable to thirteen different settings that range from 175 to around 500°F. The unit has a bright LED temperature readout for internal temp monitoring and even a meat probe.

## GAS SMOKERS

If you think the world of *electric* smokers and smoker/grillers is crowded, wait until you start to shop for your next propane (LP) or natural gas (NG) unit! We simply lost count after twenty-five manufacturers, and many of these companies that make electric smokers also have a full line of gas smokers.

As you know, the vast majority of gas smokers use propane (LP) as a fuel source. It's safe, relatively inexpensive, and readily available in everything from one-pound disposable canisters up to hundred-pounders. The most common are the familiar five-pound canisters that are available at gas stations, convenience stores, supermarkets, etc. Most all of the larger capacity smokers come with a hose/regulator system that is ready to hook up to your five-pound propane tank (or larger), while some of the smaller camping-type smokers are set up to take only the disposable canisters. Adapters to convert bulk

*Large trout fillets and other "fatty" species of fish (like salmon) can be made into great jerky with a day or two of brining before putting into the smoker. The all-time favorite for just about all fish is alder wood.*

tanks and disposable canisters to all the different smokers are available at most hardware or sporting goods stores or on-line.

If you're planning on permanently locating your smoker and don't want the yard full of propane tanks, many smokers can be converted to natural gas (NG). Some smoker makers even offer conversion kits. Check the maker's specifications, along with your local gas company.

Unlike most electric smokers, the propane models have a much greater temperature range. Low temps for jerky, smoking, and drying, and higher temps for cooking and BBQ smoking. Temps from 200–400°F are the norm. A very few (really expensive) models now even have auto start/off and temperature monitoring systems. For the most part and on most propane smokers, the gauges are pretty basic and are built around a burner that manually adjusts for low/medium/high settings only, and come with a door-mounted thermometer. On the plus side, vertical propane smokers are affordable and continue to turn out great smoked/jerked meats and other foods.

Because of the rather basic hardware and heating/burner systems, propane smokers are a lot more labor-intensive when it comes to jerky making, and you will need to figure

*In all propane smokers, you want to control the flame and keep the temperatures below 200°F so that you are drying and adding smoke flavor to your meats and snacks without cooking them. Photo by Dyna-Glo Smokers.*

*The propane smoker from Landmann Products has a two-drawer design. he top one is for the water pan, and the bottom one is for wood chips or chunks. This allows you add more wood to the smoking pan without losing heat by opening the large door.*

out the individual characteristics of your smoker system. Too hot and you are going to cook and over dry the food. Too cool and the foods don't dry properly and seem to take forever to finish off.

Several vertical propane models from the *Masterbuilt Company, Smokey Mountain* (Landmann), and *Dyna-Glo* have a two-door design in which the top door accesses the food trays and the bottom door accesses the water pan and firebox. According to the makers, this helps prevent heat loss when adding more wood by not having to open and cool down the food area.

*Weston Supply* (www.westonsupply.com) has propane vertical smokers that range in size from thirty inches to a tall forty-eight inches in height and gives the home jerky maker three to six metal racks of drying/smoking room, depending on the model. All come with a single 9,000 BTU burner and electronic lighting/ignition system. They have a fully-welded, heavy gauge steel cooking cabinet and latchable door clamps to keep the cabinet sealed tightly.

*Smokehouse Products* (www.smokehouse-products.com), long-famous for their *Lil' Chief* and *Big Chief* electric smokers, now has a propane offering in two different models. One is wide (19½ -inch wide racks) and one is narrow (11¾-inch wide racks). Both have a rotary igniter (matchless) starting system, a 14,500 BTU brass burner, four cooking grill racks, and an insulated door to add insulation and heat value to the smoker. It also makes it easier for opening/closing without burning your hands. Constructed of heavy gauge steel, the smokers have a magnetic door closure system that grabs and seals tight. Smokehouse smokers are designed to use both wood chips and chunks, and they have also have a full line of their own wood flavors.

*Camp Chef* (www.campchef.com) has both their eighteen-inch- and twenty-four-inch-wide line of *Smoke Vault* smokers. Both have a thirty-inch-high smoking/drying chamber and stand forty-four-inches in total height (including the legs). All models have a *huge* 18,000 BTU propane burner that allows you to adjust the internal temperature from a low jerky-making temperature of 160°F up to those high BBQ/smoke temperatures of 400°F.

"We know that the Smoke Vaults are a popular choice for home jerky makers," says Steve McGrath, Camp Chef Marketing Director. "In our smokers, we give you three metal racks, and one of them is mesh-designed for jerky making! We also include cooking tips, ideas, and many of our recipes."

Smoke Vaults are designed to use wood chips or wood chunks. One thing we've learned over the years of being Smoke Vault fans is the great overall versatility with wood chips or chunks that can be found with these Camp Chef products.

*Camp Chefs Smoke Vaults are available in two different sizes—18-inch and 24-inch. Both have a matchless ignition system and an 18,000 BTU propane burner for doing everything from jerky, fruits, and veggies to large cooking and smoking foods.*

# BBQ GRILLS—GAS/CHARCOAL

When it comes to home/backyard charcoal and propane grills, these are often not the first or top choice for low-temperature drying or smoking. However, there are a few tricks and suggestions that can turn virtually any backyard grill, if it has a lid, into a pretty productive jerker or dryer. Regardless of the heat source—propane or charcoal—the key is keeping the heat in the grill low (200°F or less). A little ingenuity and you can "dry" instead of cook, and even add some smoke and wood flavor.

If you have a charcoal grill, make your briquette pile small, and place it as far away from the jerky meats or food as possible. Adjust the lid slightly off to one side, or prop it open to regulate the heat once the briquettes have burned down to nearly a white ash. It is a lot more labor-intensive, but until you decide to graduate to some sort of dedicated smoker, it's a workable alternative. And with the charcoal, you can always add a small amount of wood chips or a chunk to better give your foods that smoky flavor. While the local market sells tons and tons of briquette bags for weekend cooking and backyard grilling, you may want to check with your local sporting goods store or turn to the Internet to see the many "wood flavors" of specialized briquettes that are now available for home smoking.

*If you have a propane grill and want to convert it to a smoker, there are a host of accessory items that allow you to put in some wood chips and put the aluminum can on the hot side of the fire. Not as efficient as a smoker, but it's a workable alternative until you get hooked on smoking!*

For the millions and millions of weekend and backyard pitmasters with a hooded or closed-lid propane grill, you might be surprised that you can do a lot more than "cremate" steaks, ribs, and chicken! Years ago, we discovered it was relatively easy to turn most of these low-cost cookers into a decent smoker!

Unless your propane grill is older than dirt, or is a real inexpensive model, chances are it has at least a two-burner system and independent controls. Remember that internal temps much above 200°F will *cook*, rather than *dry* your foods, so you want to keep them below that threshold. All you have to do to is light one burner, set it on its lowest setting, and leave any other burners turned off! Once the grill is up to temp, with only one burner on, add your food to the cool side and away from the heat. To check it and manipulate it, do so by slightly opening and propping the lid up.

To add wood-flavored smoke to your foods, you have three options. The first is the oldest way, by adding a wood chunk directly onto the heated propane burner. After turning on the burner, add a chunk of wood that has been water-soaked directly on the burner. The wood will begin to smolder and smoke. It's best to add the wood chunk as you bring the BBQ up to temperature and have it smoking before you add your foods. Care needs to be taken to make sure that the wood chunk does not flare up and catch fire. While this method is effective, it is pretty much old-school and is going to leave a burned wood residue in your grill and a guaranteed mess.

One of the better and more modern ways to add smoke to the propane grill is by using prepackaged smoke cans of wood pellets, such as those that are offered from Hi Mountain Seasonings (www.himtnjerky.com). Cans of smoke come in alder, hickory, and mesquite flavors. Simply open the tin can, place it on the burner, and it smokes.

*Aluminum cans of wood pellets and great smoking flavor come from Hi Mountain Seasonings and can be added to the flame side of your grill to smoke up your meats and snacks.*

*Char-Broil company makes a combination charcoaler and propane grill for those seeking a dual fuel and cooking/smoking unit.*

A relatively new device from Smokehouse Products (smokehouseproducts.com) is a small accessory unit that produces *only* cold smoke and is called the *Smoke Chief*. It attaches to the side of almost any BBQ or grill (wood, propane or charcoal), and when fired up, it can produce everything from a little smoke to a lot of smoke, and virtually *no heat!* Think of the possibilities with smoked cheese, salts, vegetables, and fruits!

Several "big name" makers of smokers and grillers also offer a line of products that use both charcoal and propane, and these are supposed to be ideal for everything from smoking and grilling to drying foods. To date, we've not seen any models that we're overly impressed with.

When you try to make a single unit into something that *does everything*, you're likely not to do anything that works really well. Such seems to be the case with the 3-in-1 and 4-in-1 combination smokers, grillers, and BBQers. It's kind of like trying to cross a Ferrari with dune buggy. It may look good on paper, but in actual use, these units are extremely large and often resemble a charcoaler and firebox that's been welded alongside a propane grill.

Some of these are often featured at the big-box home repair outlets and are actually relatively inexpensive. However, there are numerous complaints and shortcomings in terms of their overall quality and workmanship. If you're looking for the best-of-all-worlds, do a lot of research first.

Some smokers—electric or propane—are rather large and semipermanent fixtures in your backyard and outdoor kitchen. Small charcoalers and propane grills are a lot more portable and transportable on field trips where you want to WOW your family and friends with some great eats in the great outdoors—jerky, dried fruits, veggies, and snacks.

In this category, one of the more versatile, impressive, and affordable of the portable propane grillers we have seen and tested is from the Coleman Company.

The *Coleman Company* (http://www.coleman.com) has been synonymous with and known for making great outdoor and camping gear since the early 1900s. While they have yet to come out with a dedicated wood chip smoker or wood pellet grill, some of their closed-lid propane gas grills are adaptable to making jerky with a little backyard ingenuity. Their newest offering is the *NXT* series, which are relatively small/compact and portable propane grillers and use the small one-pound disposable canisters. These are easily adaptable to the larger bulk tanks with a low-cost accessory attachment.

The *NXT200* is a foldable, wheelable, portable grill that may be a little small for making a lot of jerky at home, but it is ideal for loading up in your vehicle or trailer when it's time to head out for a camping, fishing, or hunting adventure and you want to treat everyone in camp to some fresh jerky.

It has a two-burner rating of 20,000 BTUs, which is great for BBQing at home or in camp, or simply frying an egg on top of its closed lid! Luckily, the high "grilling heat" can be easily tamed by lighting only one the burners, putting the meat on the *cold side of the grill*, and then making sure that the NXT stays in and around 200°F.

*Coleman NXT 200*

## CHAPTER 4

# KNIVES, SHARPENERS, SLICERS, GRINDERS, AND JERKY GUNS

## KNIVES AND SHARPENERS

While the selection of a smoker—charcoal, gas, or electric—is much of a personal choice for making jerky and drying meats and other foods for snacks, the use of and the selection of knives and sharpeners is absolutely *critical*, and they are going to end up being your best friends for all the processing steps. When you are cutting, slicing, or processing any meats, veggies, fruits, or other snack foods, cheap knives and dull cutlery are your ultimate enemy!

Processing any game, domestic meats, or fruits and veggies requires sharp, tried, and true knives and sharpeners. If you don't have that, you are going to spend a lot of needless time with a dull or cheap knife, trying to cut and trim. Even worse, you're going to do a horrible job of cutting and trimming, and may even end up cutting yourself. There is truth in the old saying that *a sharp knife cuts clean . . . a dull knife cuts the user!*

Knife choices can range from the affordable to the *ridiculous*, in terms of costs. Knives we tested at less than $50 did as well as high tech gourmet offerings at $300 and more. They didn't have the high-cost brand names, but the steel was stout, they sharpened easily, and were affordable for most of us.

Our feeling is that the best knife is a sharp knife, and one that holds its edge. Outside of that, it has to fit your hand,

*The Game Processor kit from Outdoor Edge comes with four of the most practical knives for butchering and home-processing your meats. Knives and other accessories come packed in an easily stored hard plastic case so that everything can stay together.*

*The SwingBlade from Outdoor Edge is unique knife design that features a gut-hook for helping with the field dressing, as well as a regular knife blade that can swing into place for butchering and cutting.*

feel good, and can easily be sharpened when it dulls out. Among the knives and knife/game processing sets that we tested and used was the Game Processor set from the Outdoor Edge (www.outdooredge.com) group. Four very practical knives (caper, boning/fillet, gut-hook skinner, bowie-style butcher), along with a bone/wood saw, hand-held sharpener, brisket spreader, disposable gloves, plastic cutting board, carving fork, and game shears are all packaged in a hard-side carrying case. Knives have a full-tang construction with high-carbon 420 stainless steel blades. It's something that should be in every sportsman's vehicle when heading out for a hunting or fishing adventure, and it is ideal for processing game and fish from the field to the freezer!

Two other innovative knife designs from Outdoor Edge are the SwingBlade and the Razor-Blaze.

The SwingBlade is like having two knife types in one. It has an overall length of just over eight inches, and a drop-point skinning blade of 3.6 inches. What makes it unique for game cleaning in the field is that you simply push the lock button and the blade changes to a gutting blade/hook. It's an international knife design combining the design efforts of Outdoor Edge president David Bloch, EKA Knives of Sweden (founded in 1882), and professional Swedish hunter Thomas Ekberg.

For those who don't want the hassle of sharpening their knife, either in the field or while processing game, take a look at the Razor-Blaze with a replacement razor blade system. Push the lock button to remove and insert a shaving-sharp new blade when the old one dulls out. You can also sharpen the old blades if you want to. Knife comes with six replacement blades and a nylon sheath.

If you're searching for very high-quality American-made knives that are practical for game and fish processing in the field as well as at home, check out the offerings from *White River Knife & Tool* (www.whiteriverknives.com). Their offerings are more expensive than others; however, the workmanship is unequaled, and quality rates a solid 100 percent. They will likely be the last set of knives you will purchase in your lifetime, and all their knives come with a lifetime guarantee.

For in-the-field use, the crowning jewel in the White River Knives line is the eight-inch *Sendero Bush knife*. "We were honored to collaborate with Master Bladesmith Jerry Fisk, MS," says John Cammenga, president of White River Knife & Tool. "Jerry designed, field tested, and has been personally involved in all decisions related to the making of these knives. Mr. Fisk describes this knife as 'the best overall using knife I have made in an outdoors knife.'"

Each knife is precision ground, hand finished, and leather honed. We passed the Sendero Bush knife around while field dressing and skinning an elk, and practically had to *frisk* several members of our hunting party to get the knife back!

For deboning big game, or filleting a mess of fresh-caught fish, check out their line of a dozen different filleting knives in various blade lengths, shapes, and unique hand-fitting designs. Their six-inch traditional cork handle fillet knife has a blade that sharpens easily, and is both thin and flexible for whacking fish or doing fine deboning on game animals.

# SHARPENERS

Fresh out of the box or sheath from the knife maker every knife has a razor-sharp edge. While the knife's steel type and hardness rating certainly come into play about its overall quality, trying to guess how long it is going to stay sharp depends a lot on what the knife is cutting and being used for. Steel, carbon, and even ceramic knives get dull when used; it's as simple as that.

And while there are some great ceramic blade knives out there, all with the promise of staying sharper for ten to one hundred times longer than steel, these too have some shortcomings. They are great for slicing, but don't work well for chopping and hacking in field conditions. The blades, which are made from zirconium oxide or zirconia, are extremely hard and wear-resistant. In fact, they're almost as hard as a diamond. However, hardness does not mean that it is unbreakable. Ceramic blades don't bend and flex well, and aren't mean to whittle away on hard or semi-frozen foods, bones, or anything that isn't easily sliced. If dropped on a rock or other hard surface, they can break or chip. In addition, to return the blade to its original sharpness, it really needs to be sent back to the maker or taken to a ceramic-sharpening specialist.

So, this is why, along with your steel blade knives, a quality knife sharpener can be a great asset! Get a cheapy, and you're likely to find that using a stone ax or a broken soda pop bottle is going to produce better results when processing everything from meats and fish to fruits and veggies! Kind of like choosing a good set of knives, you most often get what you pay for. You don't have to go crazy, but we've had sharpeners that leave the blade's edge duller than when we started to sharpen it. For many people, resharpening a dull knife blade is akin to voodoo or black magic, when in fact it's like any skill—it takes a while to learn it!

When it comes to handheld/manual models, the four basic types of field and home sharpeners are carbide, ceramic, diamond, and Arkansas stone. Each has its advantages and disadvantages, and each is unique in terms of skill/sharpening expertise and practice.

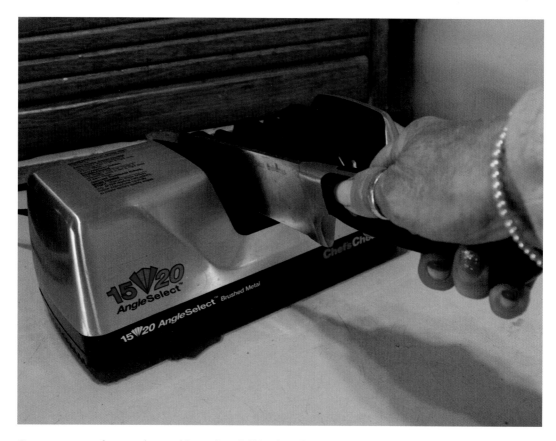

*Processing meat, fruit, and vegetables with a dull knife is dangerous and is going to mess up your snacks. The Chef's Choice Angle Select sharpener works great with all metal cutlery and allows you to choose what sharpened angle (15 or 20 degrees) you want on your blades.*

There are lots of Internet-based instructional videos showing how to successfully sharpen knives in the field or at home.

A few of the easiest handheld, inexpensive tungsten carbine sharpeners for field or light home use have been around for years and years, and come from Smith Products (www.smithsproducts.com), and Lansky Sharpeners (www.lansky.com). Their in-the-field versions won't put a precision/razor angle on your blades, but will get you out of the field and back to home where you can better hone them.

Moving up to the electric sharpeners designed for home use, as well as making your life much easier when processing a lot of fish, game, and other foods, are models with single/double carbide wheels, diamond and ceramic discs, adjustable blade angles, and much more. Unless you are planning on opening up a prime rib carving station or sushi restaurant, simply look for a good quality sharpener with a good brand name. A variety of models that are engineered and then assembled here in the US come from Chef's Choice (www.chefschoice.com). They are highly rated by many pro chefs and sportsmen.

Most sharpeners from Chef's Choice have sharpening discs that are fixed at a preset 20-degree angle. This is pretty much the accepted industry standard for home knife sharpness. A few sharpeners even allow the user to manually adjust the blade angle/sharpness. Our test unit from Chef's Choice (Model 1520) had 100 percent diamond abrasives and patented flexible stropping/polishing discs for the 20-degree angle sharpening, and a second wheel/disc that is designed for what the manufacturer terms Asian knives. It's a fancy way of allowing the user to put a 15-degree, *razor-sharp* angle on the knife.

*Small, plastic handheld knife sharpeners are great in the field when cutting and slicing, but are not a top choice for home meat processing. Processing and slicing lots of jerky meat requires a sharp knife and lots of sharpening.*

**15–17° Angle**: A severe angle that is recommended for razor blade knives and sushi-type blades. It provides an extremely sharp but delicate edge that dulls quickly and requires frequent sharpening.

**20–25° Angle:** A commonly used angle for most blades used for kitchen cutlery and filet/boning knives.

**25–30° Angle:** This is the industry recommended angle for most knives that need a more durable/heavy use edge.

## MEAT CUTTERS/SLICERS

When you finish processing any big game animal (chunking, steaking, trimming, deboning), you've once again discovered just how much work has gone into the initial preparation for making jerky. Add to this that if you plan to put up a bushel or more of fruits and vegetables for drying or dehydrating, there is still the daunting and time-consuming task of slicing the foods to the recommended thickness for proper smoking and drying.

Hand cutting meats, fruits, and veggies to that thickness of around ¼-inch is a real pain, and slices are never exact, unless you have a meat or food slicer! Pulling a big roast out of the freezer, letting it semi-thaw, then putting it into your slicer makes the task easy, with uniform thickness/cuts and the option of round medallions of meat instead of long sticks. *Never try to slice the meats if they are totally frozen. Let it thaw* on the kitchen counter for a couple of hours or semi-defrost it in your microwave. On the flip side, it's not a good idea to try to slice meats that are simply chilled or at room temperature. You can "harden" up the meat slightly by putting it in the freezer for 20–30 minutes before slicing. Room temperature/raw has a tendency to not slice cleanly and can gum up the slicer blade.

If you plan on just making jerky on a regular basis, Weston Supply (www.westonsupply. com) makes a manual and dedicated jerky slicer that is unique and inventive. Their hand-crank slicer bolts to any table, stands seventeen inches high, and has thirty-two super sharp stainless steel rotating blades that are designed to slice through the toughest cuts of meat! Two steel combs guide the meat and prevent jamming as you drop up to a 4½-inch wide and 1¼-inch thick chunk of meat into the top of the unit. Simply turn the crank handle a couple of times, and out come fifteen strips of meat all cut to ³⁄₁₆-inch slices that are ready to marinate or cure for the smoker, oven, or dryer. Weston also offers an accessory meat tenderizer blade system for cubing/tendering, so that you can turn some of the meats into cuts for chicken-fried steaks.

The RedHead Pro Electric slicer (www.basspro.com) is exactly that! It is a large, heavy-duty slicer designed for processing lots of large roasts or cuts of meat as well as bushel baskets of fruits and veggies. It has an aluminum and stainless steel body and carriage, with an 8.6-inch blade and a high torque motor. The thickness control knob is easily accessible and is adjustable from 0 to 15mm (over ½ inch).

Hand-slicing the roasts, steaks, and chops processed from an elk quarter took over two hours, even after all the hand trimming! With the Pro Electric slicer, all the meats were sliced into medallions and traditional jerky strips in less than twenty minutes!

The Chef's Choice (www.chefschoice.com) VariTilt #645 slicer is a high-grade model that features a unique food carriage that operates in the traditional horizontal (flat) mode, or it can be tilted/angled up to 30 degrees to give you the option of a gravity-fed incline. The food carriage

*Slicing your meats and snack foods to precise thicknesses is easy with the RedHead Pro Electric Food Slicer we used from Bass Pro. It has a powerful motor and a large 8.6-inch stainless steel blade. Slicer is adjustable from 0-15 mm thicknesses.*

also retracts fully, when you need the additional room for slicing extra large roasts and other big cuts of meat.

The gravity feed feature is particularly helpful when slicing veggies and fruits. Set up in this position, the food slides down and self-feeds. When slicing fifty pounds of overly ripe tomatoes we were readying for the smokers, it quickly and precisely cut them to the needed ¼-inch thickness without damaging the slices and leaving us with what would have otherwise been a real gooey mess! The slicer's open design also allows you to use large trays and platters to catch the foods directly under the blade.

Safety features on the Chef's Choice slicer includes a hidden childproof switch that prevents the slicer from being accidently turned on, and an automatic on/off switch plate on the food carriage so the slicer shuts off as soon as your hand releases pressure. This is different than most of the other slicers, and does takes a little bit of getting used to.

## GRINDERS AND SAUSAGE STUFFERS

While processing any big game, the trimmings and scrap meat do not make good jerky. It does, however, make for great ground meat or snacking sticks if you take the time to grind these leftovers. The ground meats are easily processed into snacking sticks or strips with your favorite spices and are easily stored in vacuum sealed bags or canisters, just like jerky.

If you don't plan on making a lot of ground meat sticks or strips on a regular basis, you can probably get by with one of the old-fashioned hand-crank grinders like your grandma had. They haven't changed much since invented back in 1845 by Karl Drais, and still can be found in many kitchens today.

However, if you are planning on making snacking sticks, homemade sausage, or the always popular dried summer sausages with your leftover meats, it might be wise to invest in a more modern electric grinder, sausage stuffer, and snack stick maker.

As in selecting nearly any home appliance, the offerings for meat grinders can run the gamut from cheapy/toy-like versions to hard-core pro models. Our suggestion is to look for a grinder that has

*We make jerky and snackin' sticks, but a lot of folks like to make sausage. Some models like this one from Weston Supply are huge!*

plenty of grinding power! Some offerings have underpowered subpar motors with as little as 180 watt/120 volt motors. At the other end of the spectrum, some feature 1,000 to 2,000 watt/120 volt motors that are rated to even grind soft bones. Why you would want to grind bones into your jerky snacks though is beyond our comprehension!

A good mid-priced grinder that comes with a few sausage stuffing accessories is the Weston #8, which has 575 watts of power and three stainless grinding plates for fine, medium, and course grinds. In our processing, we used the coarse grinder plate for the initial grinding, and then ran the meats through a second time with the medium grinder plate. Another nice feature is that all the attachments store away in the meat stomper, so they're not scattered around the kitchen and are handy when needed.

If you are planning on making meat snacks with *casings*, look for "stuffing funnels" that squirt out the seasoned meats with a diameter of around 12–19mm. If you are going for dried summer sausage rolls, you may want to opt for a funnel of around 30mm.

## JERKY GUNS AND SHOOTERS

Whether you are going to grind your own meat, or use ground meat from the grocery store or the butcher, one of the best accessories you can have on hand is a ground meat jerky gun or jerky meat shooter. They look a lot like a home caulking gun, and actually work in a similar fashion. Once your meats are seasoned, you simply load up the meat tube, attach the round or flat shooter nozzle, and gently use the gun's handle to squirt your meat onto the smoking or dehydrating trays. These nozzles can also be used to squirt the meat into casings if you plan on making "round snacks."

Some of the guns are sold individually, while others are sold as kits that come complete with meat seasoning packages to help you get started. Some are made of plastic and pretty inexpensive, while others are

*Smokehouse Products has a full line of jerky and meat snack products and accessories that include the Little and Big Chief smokers, jerky guns, and a full line of jerky rub/mix flavors.*

metal and are more heavy-duty than commercial caulking guns! Check out all the various models that are offered by Smokehouse Products, Weston Supply, and Hi Mountain Seasonings.

*This jerky was made using a flat shooter nozzle.*

*Some fruit and vegetable dried snacks are humidity sensitive, and will actually reabsorb moisture from the air soon after coming out of your dehydrator. Store your snacks in airtight jars or ziplock or vacuum sealed bags for best long-term storage. Photo courtesy of Weston Supply.*

## CHAPTER 5

# JERKY/SNACK STORAGE AND VACUUM SEALERS

## DRIED FOOD STORAGE

While many of your food offerings are likely to be gone from the oven, smoker, or dehydrator before they cool back down to room temperature, being able to store, preserve, and keep your foods for extended periods of time is of paramount importance! As with any foods—cooked or raw—leaving them out in the open and in the air is going to greatly reduce their shelf/storage life. Moisture is the enemy of jerky and dried foods.

In the old days, we'd wrap the foods in plastic wrap, butcher paper, or aluminum foil, and stick it in the refrigerator (two weeks safe storage) or the freezer (two to six

months). Or we'd store the food in twist-top Mason jars or bulky Tupperware containers and put them away in a dark corner of the pantry. With the invention of sealable ziplock plastic bags, life became simpler and saving your jerky and dried foods was easier. Unfortunately, even the high-grade commercial freezer-type bags aren't the best method for long term storing. Better than paper, foil, or plastic wraps, they are hard to make truly air-free and airtight.

*With some of the vacuum canister options that will fit and attach to our Vacuum Sealer, it's a good option to cut down on the marination time for most of your jerky strip meats.*

One of the great tech advances in food preservation for the home has been the introduction of vacuum sealers/bags that actually work—vacuum and seal! A decade ago, many of the big name brands were little more than shelf-space-eating-novelties or kitchen toys with vacuum pumps that were weak and wore out quickly. In the simplest of terms, vacuum sealers are supposed to work by pulling air and moisture away from the jerky, fruits, or veggies and then creating a tight seal around the food with a hermetic heat seal on the food bag. With no air or moisture around the food, it means that the problem of microbes, mold, mildew, and bugs is eliminated, and neat little vacuum-packaged foods have a greatly increased shelf life. It's also a great way to store many types of food and to prevent freezer burn!

Once vacuum-sealed, you can literally throw your jerky, meat sticks, snacks, nuts, fruits, and veggies into the freezer for a year or more, with little damage to any of the food products. When it comes time for use, simply toss the package into the home microwave for 15–30 seconds. It only helps defrost, but will soften the jerky up slightly.

Hard-core commercial/industrial vacuum sealers can cost upward of $750–$3,000, and are designed for packaging airtight foods and snacks found in the grocery markets and convenience stores. Today, vacuum sealers are available from all the big-box stores, hardware outlets, sporting goods retailers, and dozens of companies on the Internet. Prices vary greatly, but some of those big-name brands continue to grind out and offer cheap low-vacuum power units that likely won't last for long.

We've gone through a half-dozen of these units, and in addition to rotten customer service, you're going to find that getting any sort of replacement parts or repairs to be impossible! When you are putting up lots of foods, having the sealer "quit sucking and give up the ghost" is anything but ideal.

*The Nesco sealer is a low-priced vacuum sealer bag unit that is good for light to medium home use sealing. It has enough suction power to crush a can, but with no internal cooling fan, the unit can overheat after a few uses and make you wait until it resets.*

Cheapy handheld valve sealers that work off batteries may be a handy kitchen gadget, but are not much of a real meat, vegetable, and fruit processing tool. Instead, shelf-top sealer appliances (with or without bag/roll storage) are the top choice. While a lot of makers don't openly advertise the power of their vacuum sealers, it's worthwhile to check and confirm it. Vacuum strength is measured in inches of mercury (inHg). The higher the number, the more vacuum or suction power. Some units are as low as 11 inHg, and as high as 28.5 inHg. Stronger suction goes hand in hand with larger motors and will likely keep your food freshest for the longest periods of time as there is less air and moisture in the bags

It isn't the most expensive or fancy sealer on the market, and that's a good thing, but the *Nesco VS-02* (www.nesco.com) receives good marks for being an inexpensive, compact unit that's designed for light vacuum sealing jobs. No rating on its vacuum pump, but it is advertised that it can vacuum and crush a soda can. Guess what? We tried it, and it can.

Nesco's sealer is fully automatic, features one-touch operation, and shuts off and seals the bag when the unit senses that all the air has been removed. It also features a manual seal-only switch that enables the user to stop the vacuuming process and eliminates the crushing of delicate foods, or poking holes in the bags with dry jerky meat edges. The sealer has a built-in roll storage compartment and bag cutter so that sealer bags can be cut to needed lengths. The VS-02 works well with any/all brands of pre cut or roll bags, and also works with their optional vacuum canisters. It has a rather small 130 watt/120 volt motor, and this results in occasional overheating, which causes the unit to shut down. You are going to have to wait a few minutes for it to cool down if trying to seal multiple bags at a time. No rapid successive vacuum/sealing with this unit, but after cooling down, it springs back to life.

Weston Supply (www.westonsupply.com) offers over a half-dozen vacuum sealer models, and overall they rate as being some of the most powerful vacuum/suction units on the market today for home use. All but their low-end models come with an internal vacuum pump that's equipped a fan-cooled motor to keep the sealer from overheating when doing a lot of repetitive sealing. That is a giant plus!

For light to medium use, check out the Realtree Outfitters Sportsman's Advantage model that has a 210 watt/120 volt motor and a vacuum pump that delivers 23 inHg of vacuum suction. The unit has a one-touch auto mode for vacuuming and sealing, along with a manual seal mode that lets you control vacuum pressure when sealing soft foods. The sealer also has both an accessory and a marinate mode. When used with the optional canisters, you can seal your foods for later use, or you can use the canisters to actually marinate and infuse your marinade/wet brine into your foods. It's a nice feature and a time-saver!

The latest innovation from Weston Supply is their new Pro-1100 sealer. What makes it a standout in their line is that this model comes with lots of power, and for the first time with any of their units, it has an internal bag-roll holder and bag cutter! This means no more fumbling with scissors and trying to cut a real straight edge, or being locked in to use pre cut bag sizes only. In addition, the Pro-1100 has a 680 watt/120 volt motor and 28.5 inHg of vacuum/suction power. Many of the much more expensive sealers that are designed for "commercial food sealing" don't offer this much power!

A last word of warning, when it comes to vacuum sealer bags: Once again, all are not created equally. Some bags are as thin as bread bags (1.5 mil) thick. Many of the bargain brands are only 2.0 mil thick. If you get a good seal, those will probably work for you; however, when working with dried meats and other foods, you'll often find they have sharp and ragged edges that will literally puncture and put microscopic holes in those bags! With those holes, it will not seal/vacuum properly.

*Any and all spices can be mixed or blended together with your meats and allowed to marinate in the refrigerator for twenty-four hours or more in a plastic bag to infuse the best and most flavor. However, a vacuum sealer system can greatly reduce that time down to an hour or two. Some vacuum sealer systems have vacuum canisters available as an accessory option.*

Look for bags that are a minmium of 3.0 mil thick. Some bags can even be up to 5.0 mil thick. However, many vacuum sealers are advertised as being able to use "any textured" commercial bags and unfortunately this is not the case. Most makers suggest that you use only their brand. For the most part, buy your replacement bags in moderation, try a few different brands, and see what works best in your own sealer.

# CHAPTER 6

# SAVORY ACCESSORIES

When it comes to accessories for your jerky and dried food preparation needs, you're going to find—like recipes themselves—you are limited only by your imagination. Much like deciding what options and features you want when ordering a new vehicle, it comes down to personal preferences and your budget. In a generic sense, a good cutting board is an obvious choice as an essential accessory. Insulated gloves, for dealing with hot woods, smokers, and ovens are another one of those "must have" items.

*Many fruits and vegetables that require overnight to twenty-four–hour marination to infuse flavors are ideal candidates for use in the Marinade Express vacuum/tumbler. Liquid-based marinade flavors can be sucked into your raw snacks in less than an hour.*

If you are planning on making or using a lot of marinades or wet brines to add infused flavors to your meats or vegetables, and don't want to put your foods in sealable bags and have to wait twelve to forty-eight hours, a vacuum machine is a great way to quickly pull your flavor juices into your foods. Some of the commercial/home vacuum sealer systems that are used to seal up your final product also feature canister accessories that can draw the air out from around your meat, fish, and veggies to help draw your liquid marinade into them.

One product worth noting is a tabletop flavor infusion system called the Marinade Express (www.marinadeexpress.com). Some feel it almost looks like a rock and gem tumbler. It is, however, a revolutionary vacuum device that was originally developed for the restaurant and supermarket industry and has been in use for over twenty years. Up to five pounds of meats, fish, or veggies go into the large canister, and you can then use any of their eighteen dry flavoring marinades that mix with water, or you can get creative and come up with your own.

After vacuuming out the air, the canister is placed on the rotating tumbler and allowed to spin for anywhere from a few minutes to ninety minutes. Unseal the canister, remove your foods, and you are ready to head to the smoker, dryer, or home oven. What used to take one to two days now takes minutes!

While dehydrators are great for drying foods and removing moisture, they don't do anything to add additional flavor to meats, fish, fruits, or veggies. And if you don't have a traditional smoker, or don't want to mess with having to fire up all the backyard gear, short of adding liquefied smoke flavoring to your brine or marinades, there's been no way to get any sort of great wood smoke flavoring into your foods—until now!

A new product called the Smoke Chief, from the makers of the Little and Big Chief Smokers (www.smokehouseproducts.com), makes it drop-dead easy to add real wood smoke and lots of flavoring to virtually everything! The unit is small, compact, and connects temporarily or permanently to just about any grill, smoker, BBQ, charcoaler, or outdoor cooking device and quickly produces a steady stream of "cold smoke" to your foods.

The unit operates on 110 volt AC or 12 volt DC, so you can use it at home and in the field. One cup of wood pellets will provide smoke up to about three hours of steady smoke to your foods. We found it ideal for adding smoke to fish and jerky meat when it wasn't practical to use a traditional smoker. It was especially useful when the outside temps were *sub zero* and it was easiest to make the foods or jerky that is smoked, and finish them off inside the house in the dehydrator or kitchen oven. It also was great for adding smoke flavor to thin sliced tomatoes, onions, almonds, pumpkin seeds, and all sorts of cheeses!

# CHAPTER 7

# MARINADES, RUBS, SPICES, CURES, SEASONINGS, AND BRINES—IT'S THE SOUL OF THE JERKY

While all the world of adding flavor to your jerky treats and other dried snacks may sound confusing and overwhelming, the truth is you can add layers of taste, zest, sweetness, tang, salt, heat, umami, and much more by keeping it pretty simple. A lot of it comes down to personal flavor tastes and a little imagination.

Beginning with the basics when it comes to strip meat, ground meat snacks, fish, and poultry jerky, you want to add or infuse salt as both a flavor and drying preservative. While not required most jerky makers are going to want to add in flavor—everything from mild to wild! As you go through all the recipes we're presenting here, it should be obvious that all of them are designed to be "tweaked" to your tastes. That is the beauty of being the chef in control and the jerky master.

For the majority of the jerky meat making, you will likely be using what is commonly called a dry or wet cure. It's as simple as using a curing salt and one or more of your favorite spice flavors that can be dry or mixed with liquids. Curing salts are typically a combination of salt and sodium nitrate or sodium nitrite that not only help kill bacteria, but also give meats a pinkish or red color. If purchased "raw" it is often pink in color, so that it can be distinguished from ordinary salt.

*Check out your sporting goods store or go onto the Internet, and you will be overwhelmed with the number of and flavors for cures, rubs, marinades, and brines for making everything from jerky strips and snackin' sticks to poultry and fish. Shop sparingly until you find the brands and flavors you like best, or pick your favorite recipe and mix your own spices.*

Some call this process marinating, but in a more true sense the process of marination is using spices in combination with acids (vinegar, lactic, citric), oils, wine, soda pop, beer, or even milk that add flavor and break down connective tissues

Almost all of the commercially produced jerky cure and seasonings have taken the guesswork out of this curing process. Hi Mountain Seasonings (www.himtnjerky.com) has over eighteen flavor/cure offerings to make the home process of all the jerky meats a simple process.

"Over the years, we've developed our dry cures and seasonings to be nearly fool proof," says Hans Hummel of Hi Mountain Seasonings. "Whether you are doing muscle meat or ground meat strips, you simply weigh how much meat you are planning on making, and add the right about of flavoring and the cure salt. After that, your meat goes into the refrigerator or iced up cooler, in a plastic bag or container, and marinates overnight or up to twenty-four hours."

As a general rule to follow, allow the wet or dry cure on your meats plenty of time to permeate the protein cells. We find the best results by going at least twenty-four hours, as most of the cures and seasonings saturate through the protein cells at a rate of ¼-inch for each twenty-four–hour period.

For fish and poultry, there are also plenty of wet brine options. Brine uses a salt, water, and sometimes a flavor combination (honey, sugar, molasses, garlic/herbs) that forces the solution into the protein cells via the process of osmosis. A good soak for twenty-four hours in the refrigerator on your fish or poultry fillets or strips will infuse a salty flavor before you start smoking and drying. Once your fillets or strips are air-dried (sixty minutes) you can add an additional layer of flavor to the meats by adding a fish or poultry rub or basting on more spices.

*Adding flavor to your jerky is sometimes as easy as opening up a seasoning packet! Taco, Italian salad dressing, and even French onion soups mixed with water or beer are the basis for some great marinating.*

Infusing the cures/seasonings and the brines can be sped up with some specialized equipment. Some of the home vacuum bag sealer systems do a fair job, and come with vacuum canister options that will help pull out the air and infuse your liquid solution mix. If you're planning on becoming the backyard jerky master, the Marinade Express (www.marinadeexpress.com) is a tabletop appliance that not only vacuums in the flavors, but tumbles your meats and veggies for added coverage and deeper penetration.

Rubs, dry seasoning, or a wet basting are applied after the curing or brining process.

*Depending on your tastes, most all of the popular oriental sauces and spices blend well with nearly all kinds of jerky meats including pork, beef, big game, fish, and poultry.*

Some of the more popular additions that are likely to be found in nearly everyone's pantry include: ground black pepper, soy sauce, Worcestershire, ponzu sauce, honey, crushed brown sugar, maple or boysenberry syrup, mustard, catsup, BBQ sauce, teriyaki sauce, garlic/onion powder, chili/cayenne powder or flakes, your favorite hot sauce (Cajun or sriracha), powdered taco seasoning, dried French onion soup mix, lemon pepper, cumin, sesame oil/seeds, ginger, garam masala (Indian spice), dried ranch dressing mix, steak sauce, hoisin (Chinese BBQ sauce), harissa (Moroccan spice rub), fish sauce, dry sherry, wine, vermouth, and even bourbon!

Remember what we said about using a little imagination? Just make sure that as you experiment with different flavors, rubs, seasonings, and spices, you make notes on your most successful meat treats. You might have that anyway—the important thing is that you can re-create the good ones.

# CHAPTER 8
# WOOD TYPES FOR SMOKING FLAVORS

Marinades, brines, rubs, and spices may be the heart and soul of making great jerky and snacks, but the wood smoke is the icing on the cake! The beauty of wood chips, pellets, and chunks is that there are so many types and flavors to select from and use in your electric or propane smoker.

When it comes to wood types and flavors, one of the best guidelines to follow is, "less smoke is often more, and enough is really enough!" One of the biggest mistakes smoke chefs can make is in over-smoking everything from jerky to fruits and vegetables.

*Wood pellets, chips, and chunks come in a wide variety of flavors. Fruit woods give your jerky and snacks a sweeter flavor, while hardwoods are more bold.*

Simply put, too much smoke makes your foods bitter, and they can end up tasting like you are eating leftovers from the bottom of the fire pit!

For smoking and different wood flavors, the hardwood trees and the deciduous woods (the ones that seasonally lose their leaves) are the best. These include almost all the fruit and nut trees. These are the woods that have great flavor, smoke slowly, and in scientific terms, have a compact cell structure. The other, softer woods, like pine, fir, spruce, redwood, hemlock, and cypress, are all evergreens, or coniferous trees (do not lose their leaves). These are the woods that actually have more air in the wood cells, and when burned/smoked for flavoring or drying, they have a more pungent sap, and these woods burn fast. Don't use them! Also, never use any lumber, wood scraps, or treated woods! Some might even poison your food with really bad smoke that will make you sick.

Be smart, and choose your smoking wood types and flavors carefully, selectively, and in moderation.

For the vast majority of the electric and propane smokers in the marketplace for home use today, wood chips, wood chunks, and wood pellets are the most popular and easily accessible for the home jerky master and food smoker. Most common commercial chip, chunk, and pellet flavors are alder, apple, cherry, hickory, maple, and mesquite. And while there are dozens and dozens of other woods that are good or even great for smoking, most of those flavors are not readily available from all of the major sporting goods outlets. Most of the common woods cover the gamut of good flavors for all of the recipes we've provided. If you are looking for other flavors, simply do a search on the Internet. There are many exotic and unusual offerings from small suppliers around the country.

**Alder:** It is a delicate hardwood with a subtle sweet flavor. It works great for fish and poultry jerky. It's also a favorite for smoking just about every variety of nuts.

*The Smoke Chief from Smokehouse Products is a small, portable cold smoke unit that can be attached to just about any BBQ or grill. It uses a cup of wood pellets, smokes for up to three hours, and adds flavor to any meats, veggies, fruits, or cheeses.*

*Apple:* It is a very mild fruit tree wood that's great for fish, poultry, red meats, ham, luncheon meats, fruits, and vegetables. It's a favorite wood for cold smoking and making smoked cheeses.

*Cherry:* While it is a sweet and fruity wood, it is bolder and stronger in flavor than most of the other fruit woods. For jerky it's a great choice for any of the red meats—strips or snack sticks.

*Hickory:* This wood is slightly sweet and imparts more of a strong bacon-like flavor. Works great on all red meats, and is a top choice for making wild boar, bear, and other critter jerky.

*Maple:* It's a wood that is mild and also has a slightly sweet flavor that works well with poultry jerky. It's also a good choice for smoked vegetables and cheese.

*Mesquite:* This wood is "king of the hill" when it comes to having a strong and hard-core earthy flavor. It works well with all red meats, duck/goose, and fish jerky, but can be a little overpowering for lighter meat game birds and poultry.

## WET OR DRY WOOD AND THE MAGIC TEMPERATURE

While some jerky masters swear that soaking their wood chips and chunks before putting them in the smoker is mandatory, we'd respectfully disagree. Most all of the smoking hardwoods and fruit trees have enough natural moisture in the wood itself that will be released in your smoker as it heats up. In a gas/propane smoker, soaking the chips and chunks may prolong the life of the wood, but it will also take a lot longer to produce smoke! Considering that you never want a true fire in your smoke box/wood pan but instead want the chips or chunks to smolder, most of what you see when using wet wood is water vapor and steam. Smoking woods add your flavor; steam does not.

And if you are using one of the modern self-loading smokers that use pellets, getting them wet will turn them into mush, and they will not load or feed through the auger systems. Keep them dry!

Once your smoker is wood-loaded and ready to fire up, for making jerky—strips or ground meat snacks—the idea is to dry and smoke, not cook, the meats! Unlike doing ribs, brisket, a roast, or a whole turkey, the secret to jerky dying success is in a low, slow, and smoky environment.

Best results for all of meats, fish, and poultry are going to bring your smoker up to a high enough temperature to start the wood smoldering. Don't worry if it reaches 300°F, as sometimes this is where many of the chips and chunks start to ignite. Once the smoke is going, simply turn the temperature control back down to a lower setting so that you can maintain a constant temperature between 175–200°F. If your smoker has a water pan, you can put it in place and let it act as a heat diffuser. It doesn't do anything in terms of lowering the smoker's temperature, but it does keep some of the direct and

*Wood pellets for your grill and smoker also come in a wide variety of flavors. Best bargain is in buying the big bulk bags and being able to rotate your favorite types depending upon what kind of meats and eats you are smoking and drying.*

hottest heat a little more diffused. Do not, however, add any liquid to the water pan, as this is going to just get hot and steam. And for drying meats, you want dry heat only.

As we pointed out earlier, too much smoke and your meats are going to be bitter. Depending on your individual smoker, usually one or three refills of the wood-smoking pan for an entire batch of jerky is going to be plenty. After a few "smoke trials" and experiments, you should be able to adjust those levels up or down to suit your individual tastes. Remember that jerky drying can run all the way from moist and bendable to rock-hard missile strips. Here again, it comes down to your personal preference. Just remember that dry, dry jerky will keep longer without refrigeration or freezing, while those softer/tender morsels of meat with a higher moisture content are best consumed in a day or two, or placed in the refrigerator or sealed up for the freezer for long-term storage.

Once you get started making your own meats, you're likely to find that long-term storage is rarely a problem, and you'll quickly discover that you probably should have doubled the recipe to begin with! Hungry family members, as well as lots of friends you never knew you had before, are likely to keep your jerky stash in short supply.

For adding some rich smoke flavor to your snacking vegetables and fruits, follow the same basic procedure in setting everything up with your smoker. However, you are definitely going to want to slow down the drying process and keep the internal temperature down to around 135–145°F. Many propane smokers are not designed to work at those lower temperatures, so a little manual manipulation may be needed. Simply try to prop open the smoker's door slightly to bring down that internal heat.

*Here you can see how the smoker utilizes the wooden pellets.*

# CHAPTER 9
# JERKY AND FOOD SAFETY

As long as people have been making jerky at home, there has been an ongoing controversy about food safety, preparation techniques, and internal meat temperatures that are needed to ensure that the products produced are safe to eat. After all, there are some pretty nasty bugs and bacteria out there. However, in all our combined eighty-five years of preparing virtually every kind of critter meat imaginable, neither of us (authors) or our friends have ever been sickened by any jerky that we have prepared.

While we all know that the government is there to help and protect us . . . many believe some of the guidelines are not only overprotective, they are unrealistic and pretty unsavory! Most protein that has been precooked before turning into jerky ends up often not taking a marinade or a brine very well, has a very different looking/eating texture, and ends up tasting like the classic rubber chicken and gray mystery meat we've all been subjected to at one time or another. Meat strips that you may want to precook (boiled or baked) to 160°F before prepping for jerky making are as follows:

*Snackin' sticks in the round are easy to make/squirt onto the plastic jerky racks. Just make sure you keep the heat at around 175°F. With most red meats, hickory, cherry, or mesquite wood flavors are the favorites.*

- Bear
- Pork
- Rabbit
- Oddball small game—such as opossum, squirrel, marmot, muskrat, beaver, raccoon, etc.

The mainstream meats used in the majority of jerky making, such as beef, lamb/sheep, goat, elk, bison, deer, antelope, moose, caribou, birds, etc., have never caused any of us any problems. However, we are not suggesting that these guidelines be ignored. We are simply saying that these are the official United States Department of Agriculture (USDA) Jerky and Food Safety guidelines and this is what they are recommending.

They were last changed/modified back in August 2013, and are presented below in their entirety your consideration. We report, you decide!

Any updates can be found on the USDA website at: www.fsis.usda.gov.

## USDA Jerky and Food Safety Guidelines

When raw meat or poultry is dehydrated at home—either in a warm oven or a food dehydrator—to make jerky which will be stored on the shelf, pathogenic bacteria are likely to survive the dry heat of a warm oven and especially the 130 to 140°F of a food dehydrator. Included here is the scientific background behind drying food to make it safe and the safest procedure to follow when making homemade jerky.

## WHAT IS JERKY?

This product is a nutrient-dense meat that has been made lightweight by drying. A pound of meat or poultry weighs about four ounces after being made into jerky. Because most of the moisture is removed, it is shelf stable—can be stored without refrigeration—making it a handy food for backpackers and others who don't have access to refrigerators.

Jerky is a food known at least since ancient Egypt. Humans made jerky from animal meat that was too big to eat all at once, such as bear, buffalo, or whales. North American Indians mixed ground dried meat with dried fruit or suet to make "pemmican." "Biltong" is dried meat or game used in many African countries. Our word "jerky" came from the Spanish word "charque."

## HOW CAN DRYING MEAT MAKE IT SAFE?

Drying is the world's oldest and most common method of food preservation. Canning technology is less than two hundred years old and freezing became practical only during this century when electricity became more and more available to people. Drying technology is both simple and readily available to most of the world's culture.

The scientific principle of preserving food by drying is that by removing moisture, enzymes cannot efficiently contact or react with the food. Whether these enzymes are bacterial, fungal, or naturally occurring autolytic enzymes from the raw food, preventing this enzymatic action preserves the food from biological action.

# WHAT ARE THE TYPES OF FOOD DRYING?

There are several types of food drying. Two types of natural drying—sun drying and "adibatic" (shade) drying—occur in open air. Adibatic drying occurs without heat. Solar drying sometimes takes place in a special container that catches and captures the sun's heat. These types of drying are used mainly for fruits such as apricots, tomatoes, and grapes (to make raisins). Sun drying is not recommended for making meat jerky due to a lack of a steady heat source and the potential for contamination from animals, insects, dust, and bacteria.

Drying from an artificial heat source is done by placing food in either a warm oven or a food dehydrator. The main components of an electric food dehydrator include:

- a source of heat;
- airflow to circulate the dry air;
- trays to hold the food during the drying process; and
- mesh or leather sheets to dry certain types of foods.

*Turkey can be precooked before marinating and heading to the smoker; however, that is going to change the texture of the jerky. A turkey breast on sale at the grocery store is a great way to do a little "home processing," and making up a lot of jerky strips.*

# WHY IS TEMPERATURE IMPORTANT WHEN MAKING JERKY?

*Nesco's flagship dehydrator is the FD2000, which comes with six mesh-screen trays and and offers over ten square feet of drying area. Everything is digital controlled with temperatures up to 160°F and a full twenty-four–hour drying timer.*

Illnesses due to *Salmonella* and *E. coli* O157:H7 from homemade jerky raise questions about the safety of traditional drying methods for making beef and venison jerky. The USDA Meat and Poultry Hotline's current recommendation for making jerky safely is to heat meat to 160°F and poultry to 165°F before the dehydrating process. This step assures that any bacteria present will be destroyed by wet heat. But most dehydrator instructions do not include this step, and a dehydrator may not reach temperatures high enough to heat meat to 160°F or 165°F.

After heating to 160°F or 165°F, maintaining a constant dehydrator temperature of 130 to 140°F during the drying process is important because:

- the process must be fast enough to dry food before it spoils; and
- it must remove enough water that microorganisms are unable to grow.

# WHY IS IT A FOOD SAFETY CONCERN TO DRY MEAT WITHOUT FIRST HEATING IT TO 160°F?

The danger in dehydrating meat and poultry without cooking it to a safe temperature first is that the appliance will not heat the meat to 160°F and poultry to 165°F—temperatures at which bacteria are destroyed—before the dehydrating process. After drying, bacteria become much more heat resistant.

Within a dehydrator or low-temperature oven, evaporating moisture absorbs most of the heat. Thus, the meat itself does not begin to rise in temperature until most of the moisture has evaporated. Therefore, when the dried meat temperature finally begins to rise, the bacteria have become more heat resistant and are more likely to survive. If these surviving bacteria are pathogenic, they can cause foodborne illness to those consuming the jerky.

# WHAT RESEARCH FINDINGS EXIST ON THE SAFETY OF JERKY?

"Effects of Preparation Methods on the Microbiological Safety of Home-Dried Meat Jerky" was published in the *Journal of Food Protection*, Vol. 67, No. 10, 2004, Pages 2337–2341. The authors are from the University of Georgia (Brian A. Nummer, Judy A. Harrison, and Elizabeth L. Andress, Department of Foods and Nutrition, and Mark A. Harrison, Department of Food Science and Technology) and from Colorado State University (Patricia Kendall, Department of Food Science and Human Nutrition and John N. Sofos, Department of Animal Sciences).

Marinating meat doesn't make raw meat safe. "Marination alone did not result in significant reduction of the pathogen compared with whole beef slices that were not marinated," concluded the study.

In the jerky studies, some samples showed total bacterial destruction and other samples showed some bacterial survival—especially the jerky made with ground beef. Further experiments with lab-inoculated venison showed that pathogenic *E. coli* could survive drying times of up to ten hours and temperatures of up to 145°F.

A study by the Harrisons and Ruth Ann Rose, also with the University of Georgia, was published in the January 1998 *Journal of Food Protection*, Vol. 61, No. 1. The authors analyzed ground beef jerky made with a commercial beef jerky spice mixture with and without a curing mix containing salt and sodium nitrite.

Half of the ground beef was inoculated with *E. coli* O157:H7 before making it into jerky strips and dehydrating it. The authors found that in both the heated and unheated samples, the jerky made with the curing mix had greater destruction of bacteria than jerky made without it. The jerky made with the mix and heated before dehydrating had the highest destruction rate of bacteria.

They concluded, "For ground beef jerky prepared at home, safety concerns related to *E. coli* O157:H7 are minimized if the meat is precooked to 160°F prior to drying."

# WHAT ARE THE USDA MEAT AND POULTRY HOTLINE'S RECOMMENDATIONS FOR MAKING HOMEMADE JERKY?

Research findings support what the Hotline has been recommending to callers. Additionally, safe handling and preparation methods must always be used, including:

- Always wash hands thoroughly with soap and water before and after working with meat products.
- Use clean equipment and utensils.
- Keep meat and poultry refrigerated at 40°F or slightly below; use or freeze ground beef and poultry within 2 days; whole red meats, within 3 to 5 days.

- Defrost frozen meat in the refrigerator, not on the kitchen counter.
- Marinate meat in the refrigerator. Don't save marinade to re-use. Marinades are used to tenderize and flavor the jerky before dehydrating it.
- Steam or roast meat to 160°F and poultry to 165°F as measured with a food thermometer before dehydrating it.
- Dry meats in a food dehydrator that has an adjustable temperature dial and will maintain a temperature of at least 130 to 140°F throughout the drying process.

*Ready-made jerky may be convenient, but it is extremely expensive! Three to four ounce packages actually add up to $30–$40 a pound or more! Using your own meats, spice blends, and even commercial cures can bring those costs down to $10–$12 a pound and provide you the chance to make a lot of your own custom flavors.*

## ARE THERE SPECIAL CONSIDERATIONS FOR WILD GAME JERKY?

Yes, there are other special considerations when making homemade jerky from venison or other wild game. According to Keene and his co-authors, "Venison can be heavily contaminated with fecal bacteria—the degree varying with the hunter's skill, wound location, and other factors. While fresh beef is usually rapidly chilled, deer carcasses are typically held at ambient temperatures, potentially allowing bacteria multiplication."

## IS COMMERCIALLY MADE JERKY SAFE?

Yes, the process is monitored in federally inspected plants by inspectors of the U.S. Department of Agriculture's Food Safety and Inspection Service. Products may be cured or uncured, dried, and may be smoked or unsmoked, air or oven dried. The following terms may be on processed jerky products:

- **Beef Jerky:** produced from a single piece of beef.
- **Beef Jerky Chunked and Formed:** produced from chunks of meat that are molded and formed, then cut into strips.
- **Beef Jerky Ground and Formed or Chopped and Formed:** produced from ground or chopped meat, molded and cut into strips. Beef Jerky containing binders or extenders must show true product name (e.g., "Beef and Soy Protein Concentrate Jerky, Ground and Formed").

- **Species (or Kind) Jerky Sausage:** the product has been chopped and may be dried at any stage of the process, and it is stuffed into casings.

## WHAT IS THE SAFE STORAGE TIME FOR JERKY?

Commercially packaged jerky can be kept twelve months; home-dried jerky can be stored one to two months.

*Prepared jerky can be stored in the refrigerator for weeks, or it will last indefinitely in your freezer until ready to use. Vacuum sealed bags (left) do a much better job of protecting and sealing out air than supermarket zip-lock bags (right).*

# CHAPTER 10
# MOUTHWATERING JERKY STRIPS

Just say the word "jerky," and almost everyone immediately thinks of chewy meat strips that are made from muscle meat, from beef or big game. It's far and away the simplest jerky any of us can make at home. It starts with a large steak, roast, or chunk of meat that is cut into strips or medallions ¼–⅜ inch thick and trimmed of gristle, fat, and other chewy parts. Trimmed up nicely, the secret to beginning to infuse great flavor is in your marinade, cure, or rub.

*Kathy Mattoon's 6x6 bull elk taken with a black powder rifle makes for a great wall mount, but even better is the idea that once processed and deboned that we're going to have 300-400 pounds of great eating meat. Friends will be standing in line waiting for elk jerky.*

One of the great joys of making homemade jerky is how you are going to be pleasantly surprised at just how well various spices and flavors actually blend well together. As with all the recipes we have tried and written up, don't be afraid to adapt and modify them to your individual tastes. Adding a little more of one spice, less of another, or trying something different and "outside the box" is part of the fun of customizing the jerky and being able to make your own secret recipe.

As you thumb through all the recipes, you are going to note that some of them come from leading smoker, grill, and dehydrator makers. What better group of folks from which to try and test their recipe offerings than the manufacturers who design, make, and sell these great products all around the world? Every recipe that appears here has been tried, proven, and sometimes even tweaked a little to improve our flavor levels and expectations.

We've said it before, but we'll say it again: Jerky meat strips, when cut to size and placed in either a dry or wet cure or marinade, will absorb flavors/spices and then cure at a rate of ¼-inch tissue penetration for each twenty-four hours. The only way to accelerate that process is by using some sort of vacuum canister system that draws the air out from around the meats and helps draw the flavor/spices into the meat cells. It works best with wet (liquid added) brines or marinades. Some vacuum sealer systems come with optional accessory canisters/cords that are designed to do this. And there are also vacuum/tumbler appliances to help speed up this process.

Some of the recipes here will also call for and suggest the use of some sort of *curing salt*. When making jerky, salt cure is a good preservative and adds longevity to the storage and shelf life of the finished strips. If we are planning on eating all the jerky soon after drying, or if you are planning on freezing it for long-term storage, the curing salt can become an option. Bulk bags of great curing salt that we recommend come from Hi Mountain Seasonings (www.himtnjerky.com), and can be ordered online from their website.

When preparing meats for jerky, beef is pretty much ready to marinate or cure right from the grocery store. Wild big game—deer, elk, antelope, moose, sheep, goat, bison, and others—are best and safest after allowing to *"hard freeze"* (0°F) for about sixty days before jerking.

Other meats such as wild hog, bear, beaver, raccoon, marmot, rabbit, and others, come with a word of caution. All of these meats are safest to eat as jerky once the internal meat temperature has reached 160°F. Heated to below that, and there is a chance that it is not safe. If you are using an oven or smoker, it's pretty easy to get the meat temp up to that safe level. If you are using a dehydrator and your unit does not heat and dry at 160–165°F, you may want to precook the meat strips by boiling (5–10 minutes) or baking (30–40 minutes) before you marinate/cure the meats and prepare them for the dehydrator.

# HI MOUNTAIN JERKY STRIPS

- 2 pounds lean beef, big game, lamb/goat, or big game meat strips (also works with turkey/poultry, game birds, and waterfowl)
- 1 tablespoon + 2 teaspoons Hi Mountain Seasonings
- 1 tablespoon + 2 teaspoons Hi Mountain Cure

Of all the "ready to use" commercial jerky making rubs and cures that are on the marketplace today, you'd be hard-pressed to find better quality and flavor selection than those from Hi Mountain Seasonings (www.himtnjerky.com). While we have dozens of recipes for making your jerky and meat sticks from scratch and your own home ingredients, sometimes you simply want to take the easy way to make great snacks. With eighteen different Hi Mountain jerky flavors, they are ready to roll out of the box, or can be modified and added to for your custom flavors—garlic or onion powder, ground black/red pepper, cumin, oregano, cloves, coriander, cilantro, and more.

Take the *weighed* meat strips and place into a plastic bag or container. Add the cure and seasonings to the meat, massage well, and let marinate/cure in your refrigerator for 12–24 hours or more. There is a dry cure/seasoning mix, so no additional liquid is required. However, adding liquids and your own touches is certainly permissible and a great way to customize the jerky to your tastes!

# BASIC JERKY—101

- 2 pounds lean meat jerky strips
- 1½ tablespoons commercial curing salt
- 2–3 teaspoons sugar
- 1–2 teaspoons ground black pepper
- 1 teaspoon garlic powder
- 1 tablespoon liquid smoke flavoring (optional)

We call this *Jerky 101*, because it is far and away the best, most basic, and greatest tasting "beginning jerk master" recipe. It is one that has been around since the cowboys. It's a great way to put up a lot of jerky in a hurry or a great starting point for the newcomer to practice with some of the fundamental flavors before going on to become more creative and experimenting with additional tastes—zesty, sweet, hot, tangy, savory, etc.

This recipe is pretty much a "dry cure" marination process, meaning that there are really no large amounts of liquids that need to be added. Simply put your meat strips in a plastic bag/container, add your spices, and mix thoroughly before putting it into your refrigerator for 12–24 hours. This allows all the cure and flavors to infuse into the meats. If you are dehydrating them, you may want to add the liquid smoke flavoring. If you are putting it in your gas/electric smoker, forego the flavoring and plan on adding "real smoke" with the addition of your favorite flavored wood type. Mesquite, hickory, and cherry wood add a bold smoke flavor.

## MILD MEXICAN MEDALLIONS

- 2 pounds lean meat—can be in strips or medallions
- 1 can of beer or 1½ cups of water
- 2–3 tablespoons of tequila (optional)
- 1 package commercial taco meat seasoning

This is a really easy recipe with a south-of-the-border attitude that has great flavor and no heat. If you want to "kick it up," you can add some ground red or chipotle peppers (½–1 teaspoon) to the marinade and let it all cure for 12–24 hours.

# WILD, WILD BRANDY

- 2 pounds lean meat strips (works well with all game meats)
- 2–3 ounces brandy
- 1 cup apple cider
- 1 cup soy sauce
- ¼ cup sugar
- ¼ cup seasoning salt
- 2 cups water or beer
- 1 tablespoon grated orange zest
- ½ teaspoon onion powder
- ½–1 teaspoon garlic powder
- 6 cloves (whole or ground)

Brandy flavor, orange zest, and the cloves combine with the other ingredients to make this jerky recipe from Smokehouse (www.smokehouseproducts.com) a sweet treat.

Mix and marinate 12–24 hours in your refrigerator. Drain marinade, but do not rinse, and allow the meat to air-dry or pat dry with paper towels. We used the Smokehouse Big Chief smoker with 3 full pans of hickory chips. Dry 12–16 hours until the meat is bendable but not super dry.

# THAI CHILI SAUCE STRIPS

- 2 pounds thin sliced meat strips—turkey works well too
- 1 cup Thai or your favorite oriental chili sauce (sriracha hot or garlic)
- ⅓–½ cup beer or water
- 2 tablespoons soy sauce
- 1 tablespoon Worcestershire sauce
- 1½ tablespoons curing salt (optional)
- 1 tablespoon minced jalapeño peppers—raw or pickled—or to taste
- 1–2 tablespoons rice or apple cider vinegar

This flavor blend is a popular street vendor offering in Bangkok, and when traveling along the highways throughout Thailand and the Far East. We've had it made from beef, pork, goat, turkey, and lamb. Green jalapeños are not what you get in Thailand, but they come close to adding heat and flavor without being overpowering and blistering. Put all the marinade ingredients in the food processor, blend well, and cure in a plastic bag/container inside the refrigerator for 12–24 hours. This recipe works well on the smoker, in your home oven, and in a dehydrator.

# HAWAIIAN HOT AND SWEET

- 2 pounds meat strips (can be used for pork)
- ⅔ cup pineapple juice
- 1 tablespoon garlic powder
- 1 tablespoon onion powder
- 2 tablespoons cracked black pepper
- 1 teaspoon or more red pepper flakes (optional)
- ½ cup brown sugar
- ¼ cup teriyaki sauce
- ⅔ cup soy sauce
- ¼ cup Worcester shire sauce
- ⅓ cup balsamic vinegar
- 1½ tablespoons liquid smoke flavoring (optional)

Considering that this recipe came from Hawaii and was originally made with pork, there's no wonder it's the pineapple flavor that makes this an island favorite. It also works great with any beef or big game muscle meat strips. With those meats they can simply be mixed together in a plastic bag and marinated for 24 hours or more.

If you are using pork, some suggest adding an additional 1–2 cups beer/water while bringing the marinade to a boil, adding the pork strips and cooking them in the marinade for about 5 minutes. Let the meat and liquid cool, place in plastic bag, and marinate 12–24 hours. Remove meat from the liquid and smoke/dry with favorite flavor of wood, or send it to the dehydrator or home oven.

# EXCALIBUR'S WESTERN BBQ

- 2 pounds lean meat strips
- 2 teaspoons salt (sea, kosher, non-iodized)
- 6 tablespoons brown sugar
- ½ teaspoon ground black pepper
- 1 teaspoon cayenne pepper
- 1 teaspoon garlic powder
- 2 teaspoons onion powder
- ⅔ cup red wine vinegar

A little tang, a little sweet, and a little heat comes with this recipe from the Excalibur Dehydrator folks (www.excaliburdehydrator.com). Mixed together and marinated for 12–24 hours in your refrigerator, the strips are ready for the dehydrator (155–165°F) or the home oven (175–200° F).

## MILD ORANGY ASIAN

- 2 pounds lean meat strips
- 2 cups orange juice (with pulp)
- 1 tablespoon fresh ginger, grated
- 2 tablespoons crushed garlic
- 4–5 tablespoons sesame oil
- 2 tablespoons honey
- 1–2 teaspoons ground cinnamon to taste
- ¼ teaspoon ground nutmeg

A sweet mandarin orange flavor with no heat or fire, that's a favorite for the kids and non-pepper bellies. If you want to kick it a notch, simple substitute chili sesame oil for the regular oil.

Mix all marinade ingredients in a food processor or blender until mixed well. Pour over chicken into a plastic bag/container and marinate 12–24 hours. A great favorite for the smoker with apple wood, or can be dehydrated or oven-dried.

## COFFEE BREAK JERKY STRIPS

- 2 pounds lean meat strips
- 1 cup brewed strong/super strong coffee or espresso, cold
- 1 cup soda pop/soft drink—cola, Dr Pepper, Mountain Dew
- ½ cup soy sauce
- ¼ cup Worcestershire sauce
- ¼ cup brown sugar
- 1–1½ teaspoon curing salt
- 1–½ teaspoons freshly ground black pepper
- 1–2 tablespoon hot sauce (Cajun, Tabasco)

While it's not going to replace that eye-opening morning cup of coffee, if you like coffee and sweet as flavors, this recipe from Traeger Wood Pellet Stoves (www.traegergrills.com) will light up your taste buds regardless of the hour of the day. Our favorite wood flavor for smoking this recipe was mesquite!

## TERIYAKI GARLIC

- 2 pounds lean meat strips
- 1 cup teriyaki sauce
- 1 cup beer or water
- 1 tablespoon minced garlic or garlic powder
- ½ teaspoon Cajun salt
- ½ teaspoon freshly ground black pepper
- ½–1 teaspoon red pepper flakes
- ½ teaspoon liquid smoke (optional)
- 1½ teaspoons curing salt

If you are going to oven-dry (175–200°F) or dehydrate (155–165°F), you might want to add the liquid smoke flavoring. If you are going to put it in the smoker, mesquite, hickory, or cherry woods are the top choices.

## VIETNAMESE SPICY STRIPS

- 2 pounds lean meat strips
- 2 large cloves garlic, coarsely chopped
- 1 stalk fresh lemongrass, trimmed, white parts thinly sliced or 2 teaspoons lemongrass paste (produce department)
- 1 teaspoon grated fresh ginger
- ½ cup soy sauce
- ½ cup rice wine (sake), beer, or water
- 3 tablespoons sugar
- 2 tablespoons Asian fish sauce
- 2 teaspoons hot red chili flakes, or more to taste
- ½–1 teaspoon curing salt (optional)

This recipe, with a few Kathy and Andy modifications, comes from Traeger Wood Pellet Stoves (www.traegergrills.com). After marinating, strips are ideal for oven drying (175–200°F) or dehydrating (155–165°F). If the meats are headed to the smoker, mesquite, hickory, or cherry woods are the top choices.

## CHIMICHURRI STRIPS—WESTON STYLE

- 2–3 pounds lean meat strips
- 1 cup fresh Italian parsley leaves
- ¼ cup fresh cilantro leaves
- 3 cloves garlic, crushed
- 3 tablespoons olive oil
- 1 teaspoon red wine vinegar
- 1 teaspoon lime juice
- 1 teaspoon brown sugar
- 1 teaspoon kosher salt
- ½ teaspoon red pepper flakes

Weston Supply (www.westonsupply.com) says that this is one of the most flavorful recipes that they have ever concocted for their dehydrators and is great for jerky makers looking for a different taste. Marinate the meat and all the ingredients in your refrigerator for 12–24 hours, and then light up the dehydrator at 145–165°F.

## BBQ BOURBON SWEET BITES

- 3 pounds lean meat strips
- 1 cup bourbon
- 2 cups catsup
- ½ cup brown sugar
- ½ cup beer, cola, Dr Pepper
- ¼ cup balsamic or red wine vinegar
- 3 tablespoons chopped garlic
- 1 tablespoon chili powder
- 2 tablespoons ground chipotle (smoked/dried jalapeños)—optional
- 2 tablespoons liquid smoke—hickory—optional
- 2 tablespoons Worcester shire sauce
- 1 tablespoon molasses or maple syrup
- 2 tablespoons whole grain mustard

The flavor is old south bourbon BBQ that can be taken to whatever heat level your taste buds like. Cut out the ground chipotle if you want savory instead of hot and spicy.

Mix all your marinade ingredients in the blender or food processor and heat to a gentle simmer for about 10 minutes. Remove from heat, and add additional beer or soda water if the mixture is too thick or syrupy. Marinate the meat for 12–24 hours in the refrigerator. If you are dehydrator drying, use the liquid smoke flavoring for additional taste. Set the dehydrator on 145–165°F till the strips bend, but don't break. If you are smoking the meats, leave it out the liquid smoke and add your own with a temperature of 175–200°F and several pans of hickory woods.

# WILD CHEFF SUGARHOUSE MAPLE

- 3 pounds lean meat strips
- ¼ cup Worcester shire sauce
- ½ cup soy sauce
- 4 tablespoons Wild Cheff New England Maple Balsamic Vinegar (can use 1 tablespoon maple syrup and 3 tablespoons balsamic vinegar)
- ½–1 cup Wild Cheff Canadian Steak Rub (ingredients include garlic, onion, bell pepper, parsley, black pepper, sea salt, demerara sugar)

Denny Corriveau is well-known and renowned as the *Wild Cheff*. In addition to teaching through television, writing, and radio, Corriveau does seminars and teaches wild game and organic cooking through his Free Range Culinary Institute. This recipe comes from him and Wild Cheff Enterprises (www.wildcheff.com) and uses a few of their specialty blend of spices. You can always try to duplicate and make a batch of your own, but why? He's been doing it since 1995 and makes it easy with his online offerings of fresh and prepackaged spices.

Denny suggests that you liberally douse your meat strips in the marinade mix and let it marinate in your refrigerator overnight and up to 24 hours. Check occasionally to make sure that the meat stays covered with marinade.

Drain marinade and ready it for the dehydrator at 155°F, for 6–12 hours.

The meat is sweet, tangy, and with his ready-made spices . . . easy!

# CORNED BEEF JERKY

- 3 pounds lean meat (bison, beef, venison, antelope, or elk)
- 1½ teaspoons dry mustard
- 1 teaspoon allspice
- 1 teaspoon ground roasted coriander
- 1 teaspoon garlic powder
- 1 teaspoon coarse ground pepper
- ½ teaspoon ground cloves
- ½ teaspoon mace
- ½ teaspoon red pepper flakes
- 1 bay leaf, crushed finely
- ½ teaspoon cinnamon
- ¼ teaspoon pink or curing salt

We have to admit it, with this recipe we were a little skeptical about how the end results would turn out. After all, great tasting corned beef (which itself can be dried into jerky-like strips) is a delicatessen delicacy that rates as a true art form.

Kathy and Andy have been known to try and arrange for a later flight out of New York, just so we had time to hit a famous deli or two for our corned beef sandwich fix!

The results of this Weston Supply (www.westonsupply.com) recipe far exceeded ours and everyone's expectations. Mixed and allowed to marinate in the refrigerator for 24 hours, the strips hit the dehydrator at 155°F until the meat was bendable and delicious!

*If you like flavorful corned beef, this is a recipe from Weston Supply that is going to surprise and delight you. It works great with beef strips as well as big game. We even tried it with goose and turkey.*

# MOROCCAN HARISSA

- 2 pounds lean meat strips
- 1–2 tablespoons ground cumin
- 1–2 tablespoons paprika
- 2 tablespoons salt (sea, kosher, non-iodized)
- 1–2 teaspoons ground cayenne pepper, to taste
- 2 teaspoons grated fresh garlic (optional)
- ⅓ cup finely chopped cilantro
- ⅓ cup finely chopped parsley
- 3 tablespoons lemon juice (fresh or bottled)
- ⅓ cup water to moisten
- 3–4 tablespoons fresh chopped mint (optional)

Harissa is a spicy and aromatic chili paste that's a widely used in North African and Middle Eastern cooking. We found a spice blend in both a dry rub and jam-like seasoning jar from cHarissa (www.charissaspice.com) that puts a Moroccan spin on the flavor.

You can use this recipe if you want to make your own harissa blend without too much fire, or you might want to try the cHarissa rub/seasoning. If you use theirs, you can eliminate all the ingredients except for the lemon juice, water, and mint.

Regardless of how you prepare your rub, mix all the spices together with the liquid in your blender or food processor and make sure that your meats get a full 24 hours to marinate in your refrigerator. Meats work well in the dehydrator at 155°F, or in your home oven at 200°F. The jerky does even better in the smoker at around 200°F with bolder flavored woods such as cherry, hickory, or mesquite.

*Ground meat snacks can be made from just about all varieties of big and small game, as well as domestic beef, lamb, or goat. We took the Moroccan ground meat snack recipe from Traeger Wood Pellet Grills and made them out of lamb. They were smoked with hickory pellets and blotted with paper towels till they were dry, bendable, and delicious.*

## CARDAMOM AND CLOVE

- 2 lbs lean meat strips (works great with beef, venison, elk, and antelope)
- 2 tablespoons balsamic vinegar
- 1 tablespoon cardamom pods
- 1 tablespoon whole cloves
- 1 tablespoon black peppercorns
- 1 tablespoon brown sugar
- 1 teaspoon seasoning salt

*Cardamom and clove combine to make a very unusual but great-tasting jerky blend for beef or all game meats. Go easy on the spices until you find your favorite taste levels. Photo by Weston Supply.*

Cardamom is a rather strong spice that is native to the Middle East and North Africa. As a spice, it's also more popular than cinnamon in Scandinavia and traces those roots back to the days of the Vikings and their raids into Constantinople. *Go figure that one out!* Today, it can be purchased in pod form where you will grind your own seeds, or as a pre-ground spice. Fresh pods have the most flavor but are not likely found in the local grocery store. It can easily be ordered via the Internet.

This recipe from Weston Supply (www.westonsupply.com) is probably one of the most unusual but great tasting jerky recipes we've ever tried. We dehydrated it at 155°F for about 5 hours, and we also snuck a batch of meat into the smoker with apple wood. Results of both were outstanding and didn't last long.

## SMOKEHOUSE KILLER JERKY

- 5–6 pounds lean meat strips (beef or any big game)
- 2 teaspoons garlic powder
- 2 teaspoons onion powder
- 5 teaspoons meat tenderizer
- 4–5 teaspoons ground black pepper
- 1 teaspoon ground mustard
- 1–1¼ cups soy sauce
- 1–1¼ cups Worcester shire sauce
- 1 cup red wine (sweet or dry)

This all-around great meat recipe comes from Levi Strayer at the Smokehouse Products (www.smokehouseproducts.com), makers of the Little Chief and Big Chief electric smokers. It is a universal recipe that has been a family staple for generations.

Mix all the ingredients and marinate for at least 24 hours in your refrigerator. Set up your smoker (Big Chief or Little Chief) with your favorite flavor of wood chips, plug in the smoker, and let it get up to its consistent temperature of around 165°F. Start smoking the meat and change out/replace the wood chips about every 45 minutes. Smoke the meat with 2–3 pans of wood until meat bends but doesn't break. This normally takes 8–12 hours. If it's cold outside and you need to retain more heat, use their Insulation Blanket, which is designed specifically for their smokers, once you are done with the actual wood chips/smoking process.

# KOREAN BULGOGI

- 3 pounds lean meat strips
- 1 cup pear nectar
- 1 cup beer or water
- ½ cup soy sauce
- ¼ cup regular sesame or hot sesame oil
- ¼ cup rice vinegar
- ½ cup brown sugar
- 2 tablespoons ground dried jalapeño or chipotle peppers
- 2 tablespoons ginger root, peeled and diced
- 3 garlic cloves, smashed (1 tablespoon minced)
- 1 tablespoon black peppercorns
- 1–1½ tablespoons curing salt (optional)

*The Weston Supply dehydrator, at 155°F for our jerky, actually put small "grill marks" on the meats. Try different recipes and in small batches to begin with, until you find your favorites and want to make much more. Remember, when experimenting with flavors, you are limited only by your imagination and personal tastes.*

Bulgogi from Korea is a restaurant favorite just about anywhere you can find it. It's juicy, sweet, and savory all at the same time. Add a little heat and it tickles all of the taste buds. With this recipe, which we've borrowed and modified slightly from Weston Supply (www.westonsupply.com), it works great in the dehydrator, your home oven, and your smoker. Marinate the meat overnight and then place into the Weston dehydrator at 155°F for about 6 hours; into the oven at 200°F for about 2 hours; or into the smoker at 200°F with a couple of pans of alder or apple wood until the meat is bendable. Don't over dry it and make it too crisp. It is best to start checking after smoking it for about 90 minutes.

# SWEET RANCHY COLA

- 2 pounds lean meat strips
- 1 can cola
- ⅓ cup rice vinegar
- ¼ cup honey
- 2 chipotle peppers in adobo sauce (canned)
- 2–3 tablespoons dry ranch dressing mix

Have a Coke and a smile with this recipe, and add a little ranch flavored dressing zing all at the same time!

Finely chop the two chipotle peppers and use an additional teaspoon or two of the adobo sauce from the can. Canned adobo is hot, so go easy on it until you figure out your heat level preference! Mix all the ingredients together and let marinate with the meat overnight in your refrigerator. Drain and dehydrate at 155–165°F, dry in the oven at 200°F, or load them in the smoker with cherry wood at 200–225°F. Meat is done when it bends and before it breaks and snaps.

# STEAK SAUCE STRIPS

- 2-pounds lean meat strips
- ½ cup A.1. or your favorite steak sauce
- ½ teaspoon black pepper
- 2 teaspoons Tabasco sauce (optional)
- 2 teaspoons liquid smoke flavoring
- 2 teaspoons Worcestershire sauce
- 2 teaspoons seasoning salt

A quick, easy and "steaky" flavored recipe from John Head at the Culinary Institute of Smoke, and the Cooking's Master BBQ Cooking School.

When you don't have time to get fancy with a lot of blended spices, all you have to do is mix the ingredients and marinate the meats for about 24 hours in your refrigerator. Strips can be oven-dried at 200°F, or placed in the dehydrator at 155–165°F. While drying, the meat can also be basted lightly with additional steak sauce.

*Fruit juices and jerky meat strips are an ideal combination for quick and easy marinating. The steak sauce was used for basting while the meat was in the smoker. Adding red pepper for some heat is optional. Simple, easy, and delicious!*

# CHAPTER 11
# GROUND MEAT SNACKIN' STRIPS

Ground meat snack sticks are a great way to clean up the leftover big game meat trimmings and parts that just really are not suitable for making jerky strips in the classic sense. It's also a great way to take just about any "on sale" cut of meat from the grocery store and have it turned into some great sticks and rounds that everyone loves to munch on without the traditional *jerky pull and chew!* If you purchase a big roast, ask your butcher if they will do the trim and grind for you. Most are happy to oblige, as long as you tell them what you are doing . . . *and bring them back a few samples to try!*

And yes, you can use commercial hamburger if you have to, but just make sure the meat is extra lean, and the fat content is as low as possible. Using 10–15 percent fat is about the maximum. Or, you can always use up and grind those leftover dove, duck, pheasant, turkey, or other game bird meats that are taking up space in the freezer. As a final option, great sticks and strips can be made with store-bought ground turkey or chicken.

Once you have your ground meat, you can go from mild to wild with various flavors and combinations. Meat snacks and sticks not only are great by themselves when spiced up and marinated, but they open the door to you adding a lot more flavor with dried and chopped fruits, veggies, mushrooms, cheeses, and more. *Just get creative and let your imagination run wild.*

The same holds true when adding flavored liquids. You can always use water, but fruit juices, beer, wine, liquor, and even soda pop can add everything from a rich savory taste to a sweetened flavor. All the popular bourbons, whiskey, tequila, rum, vermouth (sweet or dry), wines (sweet or dry), brandy, sherry, and even oddball liquor like crème de menthe, ouzo, Grand Marnier (orange), Galliano, and others are worth experimenting with! All the alcohol evaporates out, but the flavors remain!

Ground meat sticks, rounds, and strips are supposed to be "sticky" when mixing everything together, and many of us have found that using a small amount of powdered milk or buttermilk as a binder helps the meat snacks to stay together and not crumble once they have been dried or smoked. The powdered buttermilk will give the meats more of a "tangy" flavor, much like you find with aged summer sausage. Either way, it's another option and a flavor enhancer that you may want to include.

When it comes to commercial pre-mixed jerky/ground meat cures and flavors, as well as BBQ sauces, rubs, and spices, you are pretty much limited only by your imagination and your taste buds in terms of mixing and matching! For making your favorite snackin' sticks, a jerky gun, or shooter, makes it a lot easier to "squirt" your meats into flats or rounds. (Top to bottom jerky guns—Hi Mountain Seasonings, Weston Supply, and Smokehouse Products.)

For marinating, your best spice/marinating flavor will take 12–24 hours in the refrigerator. You can speed up that process to less than 1–2 hours if you have a vacuum canister system.

Nearly all the snack sticks, rounds, and flat strips can be processed in your dehydrator, home oven, or smoker. General rule for dehydrating is to set the unit between 145–165°F and dry the meat snacks until then are bendable, but don't crack and break. For the home oven, it's 200°F. And for the smoker, it's 175–200°F with your favorite flavor of wood smoke.

# HI MOUNTAIN MEAT SNACKS

- 2 pounds lean ground beef or big game meat (also works with turkey/poultry, game birds, and waterfowl)
- 1 tablespoon + 2 teaspoons Hi Mountain Seasonings
- 1 tablespoon + 2 teaspoons Hi Mountain Cure
- ½-⅔ cup of beer or water (to moisten)

Of all the "ready to use" commercial jerky making rubs and cures that are available on the marketplace today, you'd be hard-pressed to find better quality and flavor selection than those from Hi Mountain Seasonings (www.himtnjerky.com). While we have dozens of recipes for making your jerky from scratch and using home ingredients, sometimes you simply want to take the easy way to make great snacks. With eighteen different Hi Mountain jerky flavors, they are ready to roll out of the box, or can be modified and added to for your custom flavors—garlic or onion powder, ground black/red pepper, and more.

Mix the ground meat, seasoning, and cure thoroughly in a large bowl and place the mixture into a plastic bag or container. Refrigerate for 12–24 hours or more and use your jerky gun, or flatten and cut into ¼–½ inch thick strips, before placing in the dehydrator or smoker. If strips are headed to the smoker, great wood flavoring choices include mesquite, hickory, or cherry for a bold taste. You'll know the meat snacks are done when they are dry, but fairly bendable and tender. Over drying them to the point of being brittle will make them tougher to chew and you'll feel like you're gnawing on a pencil! If you're using a dehydrator, start checking on them after 5–6 hours, and after about 2 hours in your smoker.

*Pepperoni and other ground meat snackin' sticks can be made to look real professional if you want to take the time to use casings. Around here, we use our Weston Supply jerky gun with the casings for rounds as gifts, but most of the time they are just "squirted out," dehydrated, and consumed almost as fast as they are made.*

# SIMPLE SNACKIN' STICKS

- 2 pounds lean ground meat (works with turkey/wild poultry as well)
- 1½ tablespoons curing salt (optional)
- ¼ cup Worcestershire sauce
- ¼ cup soy sauce
- 1 teaspoon onion powder
- 1 teaspoon garlic powder
- 2 tablespoons catsup
- 1½ teaspoons liquid smoke flavoring (optional)

There's nothing difficult or complicated with this recipe, but it's a great way to learn the basics and a solid base for being able to expand on your "jerky master" talents and ideas. If you are going to oven-dry (175–200°F) or use the dehydrator (155–165°F), you may want to add the liquid smoke for an additional flavor level. Mix ground meat and spices, refrigerate 12–24 hours, and make into snackin' sticks or jerky meat strips. If the strips or sticks are going to the smoker, try using mesquite, hickory, or cherry wood.

# CLASSIC PEPPERONI WITH MOZZARELLA

- 2 pounds lean ground meat
- ⅓ pound finely grated mozzarella cheese (optional)
- ½–1 cup red wine (sweet or dry) or grape juice—to moisten
- 1½ tablespoons curing salt
- 1 teaspoon crushed/ground mustard seed
- ½ teaspoon crushed red pepper
- 1 teaspoon crushed fennel seed
- ½ teaspoon crushed anise seed
- ½ teaspoon garlic powder
- ½ teaspoon onion powder
- 1½ tablespoons fresh ground black pepper
- 2–3 tablespoons powdered milk or buttermilk as a binder (optional)

If you like classic pepperoni strips or sticks, leave out the mozzarella cheese. However, if you want a cheesy twist to your snacks, you won't be disappointed.

Mix all the ingredients together with the lean ground meat and let marinate in the refrigerator in a plastic bag/container for 12–24 hours. Take the meat mix and use your jerky gun to make strips or rounds, or you can lay the meat flat on a baking pan and cut into squares or strips.

If you really want to go classic with the pepperoni casings, you will need to stuff them with your jerky gun *before* allowing to marinate in the refrigerator. The 19–21mm collagen casings seem to work best.

## HAWAIIAN ISLANDS GINGER CHEW

- 2 pounds lean ground meat
- ⅓ cup soy sauce
- 2 tablespoons lime juice
- 1 tablespoon honey
- ½ cup beer or water to moisten
- 2 tablespoons fresh ginger root—finely grated
- 3 tablespoons orange liquor (optional)
- 1 tablespoon orange or lemon zest
- 2–3 tablespoons powdered milk or buttermilk as a binder (optional)

*Soy sauce is a salty great addition to many jerky strips and snackin' sticks. It's also ideal for vegetables. Ponzu sauce is basically soy with a tangy citrus flavor and adds additional taste when substituted in your recipes. Ponzu works well on fish and poultry.*

An islands favorite with a salty/ginger flavor, that actually started out with us as a poultry BBQ marinade. Combine ingredients and marinate in the refrigerator for 12–24 hours. Make into snackin' sticks or jerky meat strips. This recipe is ideal for oven drying (175–200°F), or for your dehydrator (155–165°F).

## MUSHROOM/ONION MEAT STICKS

- 2 pounds lean ground meat
- ½ cup (or more) finely chopped fresh mushrooms—portabella, morels, chanterelles, or even common button types
- ¼ cup pureed or finely chopped fresh onion
- 3 tablespoons dry red wine or to taste
- ½ cup beer or water to moisten
- 1 teaspoon garlic powder
- ½ teaspoon finely chopped thyme
- 1 teaspoon ground black pepper
- 1–2 teaspoons seasoning salt to taste
- 1–½ teaspoons liquid smoke flavoring (optional)
- 2–3 tablespoons powdered milk or buttermilk as a binder (optional)

Everyone loves the smoky flavor combination of fresh mushrooms, onions, and meats. If you are going to oven-dry (175–200°F) or use the dehydrator (155–165°F), you may want to add the liquid smoke flavoring. Leave it out if you plan on smoking the meats. Blend all the spices and liquids in your blender or food processor, then pour in with the ground meat and marinate 12–24 hours or more. Use your jerky gun or cut the ground meat into ¼- to ½-inch thick strips.

# BLACK FOREST CHERRY CHEW

- 2 pounds lean ground meat
- ½ cup finely chopped cherries
- ½–1 cup beer or water to moisten
- ½ teaspoon finely ground coriander seeds
- ½ teaspoon ground nutmeg
- ½ teaspoon cinnamon
- ¼–½ teaspoon caraway seeds to taste
- 1½ tablespoons curing salt
- 1 teaspoon ground black pepper
- 2–3 tablespoons powdered milk or buttermilk as a binder (optional)

Because this is a "sweet stick" snacking meat treat, it is ideally suited to be oven-dried/dehydrated rather than smoked, and no liquid smoke flavoring needs to be added.

# SARAH'S BOURBON JERKY AND PEMMICAN

- 2 pounds lean ground meat
- ⅓ cup Worcestershire sauce
- ¼ cup soy sauce
- 1–2 teaspoons fresh ginger (grated fine) (optional)
- 2 heaping teaspoons ground black pepper (fresh is better)
- 1 heaping teaspoon garlic powder
- 1 heaping teaspoon onion powder
- ½–1 teaspoon curing salt
- 2 tablespoons hot sauce (Cajun or oriental) to taste
- 2–4 ounces bourbon
- 1–½ tablespoons liquid smoke flavoring
- 4 ounces ground fresh almonds (to make pemmican)
- 8 ounces ground dried cranberries (to make pemmican)
- 2–3 tablespoons powdered milk or buttermilk as a binder (optional)

This jerky/pemmican recipe came through the Sarah Sticha family and has been used for generations. It tastes great as an easy-to-make ground meat medallion or flat meat stick, or can be easily modified to turn into delicious pemmican. Just finely grind the almonds and cranberries and add to the meat and spice mix. Blend everything together thoroughly, marinate in the refrigerator 12–24 hours, and then make into jerky gun sticks or flat medallions (¼- to ½-inch thick). Can be oven-dried, dehydrated, or smoked. Best wood flavor choices are hickory, mesquite, or cherry.

# TERIYAKI GARLIC & CILANTRO

- 2 pounds ground meat (works also with all ground poultry)
- 1 cup teriyaki sauce
- ¼ cup or more of fresh chopped cilantro to taste
- 2 tablespoons brown sugar
- 1 cup beer or water
- 1 tablespoon minced garlic or garlic powder
- ½ teaspoon Cajun salt
- ½ teaspoon freshly ground black pepper
- ½–1 teaspoon red pepper flakes
- ½ teaspoon liquid smoke (optional)
- 1½ tablespoons curing salt (optional)
- 2–3 tablespoons powdered milk or buttermilk as a binder (optional)
- A few drops of liquid smoke flavoring

*Two of the best and inexpensive flavor enhancers for just about all jerky types are garlic and onion. Using powder instead of garlic or onion salt lets you decide how much saltiness you want to add without it being overpowering.*

This recipe works well with nearly any kind of ground meat, so feel free to experiment. The cilantro added to the mix adds a unique and pleasing flavor combination to the finished sticks or strips. If you are going to oven dry (175–200°F) or dehydrate (155–165°F), you might want to add the liquid smoke flavoring. If you are going to put it in the smoker, the bolder wood flavors like mesquite, hickory, or cherry woods are the top choices.

# STICKY AND HOT HOT

- 2 pounds ground meat
- 3 cups light liquid corn syrup
- 1–1½ teaspoons curing salt
- 4 tablespoons salt
- 1½ teaspoons liquid smoke flavoring (optional)
- 2 teaspoons cayenne pepper
- 2 teaspoons red chili peppers, crushed
- 2 teaspoons chili powder
- 2 teaspoons mustard seed, ground
- 2–3 tablespoons powdered milk or buttermilk as a binder (optional)

*Sticky and Hot Hot snackin' strips can be tailored to set your taste buds on fire! Corn syrup adds the sweet/sticky texture, and red hot peppers add the heat.*

*Sticky and hot hot* is likely to be an understatement with this fiery recipe. Combine all ingredients and marinate for 12–24 hours. If you are going to oven-dry (175–200°F) or dehydrate them (145–165°F), you may want to use the liquid smoke flavoring. Use your jerky gun to make strips or snackin' sticks, and you can load up your smoker racks and dry with cherry, hickory, or walnut woods.

# 16 SPICE SNACKIN' STRIPS

- 3 pounds lean meat strips
- ½ cup water
- 3 tablespoons brown sugar
- 2 tablespoons salt
- 2 tablespoons hot chili powder
- 1½ tablespoons garlic powder
- 1 tablespoon onion powder
- 1 tablespoon ground black pepper
- 2 teaspoons ground cinnamon
- 2 teaspoons smoked paprika
- 1½ teaspoons ground cumin
- 1½ teaspoons ground coriander
- 1 teaspoon ground cloves
- 1 teaspoon cayenne
- 1 teaspoon crushed red pepper
- ½ teaspoon ground allspice
- ½ teaspoon ground fennel
- ¼ teaspoon ground ginger root

Okay, we'll admit it, this recipe that we tried from Weston Supply (www.westonsupply.com) seems to have everything in it but the kitchen sink! But, somehow when mixed with the ground meat and allowed to marinate 12–24 hours in your refrigerator . . . *it really works.*

You can make the strips all pretty and uniform if you use a jerky gun by simply loading the mix into the tube and using the gun to "squirt" the strips onto the dehydrator drying racks. Dry in the Weston dehydrator at 155°F until the sticks are bendable, but don't crack and break.

*The 16 Spice Snackin' Strips have just about everything mixed in with the meats that you can think of. Don't let that scare you; everything blends well.*

# LIVER STICKS

- 2–3 pounds lean ground meat
- ¼–½ pound ground liver
- 1 medium/large pureed sweet onion with juice
- 1 cup beer or water to moisten
- 1–2 shots bourbon (optional)
- 1 tablespoon ground cumin
- 1 teaspoon garlic powder
- 2 teaspoons salt (seasoned or Cajun)
- 1–2 teaspoons red pepper flakes
- 2–3 tablespoons powdered milk or buttermilk as a binder (optional)

Okay, we know that not everyone loves liver. The fact however is, if you hunt . . . you know that every big game animal has one. Here's a great way to use up beef or most big game liver stashed in the back corner of your freezer and make some great snackin' sticks without the liver flavor being overpowering.

Mix all your spices together, add your meat and liver, and mix thoroughly. Let it marinade in the refrigerator for 12–24 hours and then use your jerky gun to shoot out rounds or strips. Dehydrate at 155–165°F or oven dry at 200°F until the meat sticks are dry and bend. If heading to the smoker (200°F), cherry, hickory, or mesquite woods are the best.

*Antelope or prairie goats are sometimes shunned for being tough and gamey. Nothing really could be further from the truth, if the meat is properly prepared for everything from smoked/BBQed roasts and steaks to super tender and flavorful jerky.*

# CHAPTER 12

# JERKED FISH AND SEAFOOD SNACKS

Just about any fish or seafood can be smoked/dried and jerked. Some mainstream seafoods are best suited for smoking or drying and keeping moist, while others can be taken to the next level and turned into some great fish jerky. We've personally tried a lot more than fish, and the results are mixed. Squid, octopus, and shrimp can be jerked using some of these recipes and the turn out pretty impressive! Oysters, clams, and mussels were a disappointment once they got past the semidry state. Lobster, on the other hand, is best tried in order to see how great it turns out!

All of our recipes are going to let you take your fish to the jerky level. However, they are also ideal if you want to cut back on the dehydrating or smoker time and turn them into a more traditional smoked or moist snack.

For fish species, we've done them all—trout, salmon, bass, crappie, pike, perch, sunfish, catfish, and even the much-maligned carp! In the saltwater department, we've done tuna, swordfish, shark, rock cod, kelp bass, bonito, halibut, flounder, seatrout, and even mackerel. Each fish, be it dry or oily, can be smoked or dried if you invest the time and effort. Each fish type also is going to have its own unique flavor. Not everything in the fish jerky world has to taste like salmon!

Making your fish fillets into jerky strips or bites begins with making sure that most all of the bones are removed. Most of the time we take the skin off the fillets and are careful to try to get all the bones out.

As an added way to actually break down small bones, use your knife and make deep crosscuts all along the fillet. Not only is it good for breaking down any little bones, but as the fish dries, it opens small cut gaps and allows the fish to actually dry more evenly and faster.

All the fish types seem to do best for jerky making if they are brined with a mix of salt, sweet, and liquid as the basics. Add your own spices, rubs, and flavors once the fish are removed from the brine. Most recipes will have you marinate the fillets 12–24 hours.

Fish jerky, unlike meat jerky and snacks, does not always store well if not consumed soon after making. We suggest that all the fish jerky is always kept in the refrigerator or frozen up till you are ready to consume.

*Fresh caught Kokanee salmon caught on the Blue Mesa Reservoir with Andy Cochran (Gunnison Sport Outfitters) in Colorado are ready for the smoker. Salmon jerky from the smoker with a couple of pans of alder wood for flavoring is a favorite.*

# HI MOUNTAIN FISH BRINE

- 2–4 pounds fish fillets (any species)
- 1 pouch Hi Mountain fish brine in 1 gallon of chilled water

Hi Mountain Seasonings (www.himtnjerky.com) makes 3 flavors of fish brine that include *Gourmet Fish, Alaskan Salmon,* and *Wild River Trout.* All have their own slightly different flavor profile and are easy to use if you do not want or have the time to make your own brine from scratch.

Once the brine is mixed, simply place the fish fillets into the brine so that they are totally immersed, and refrigerate/brine for 24 hours or more. Once brined, rinse the fillets with tap water and allow to air-dry. Here is where you can now leave the fillets alone and ready them for the smoker/dehydrator, or add your own mix of spices/rubs. Some of our favorite "add on" spices include Cajun and regular seasoning salt, ground or red pepper flakes, lemon pepper, hot sauce (your favorite type), and brown sugar.

Dehydrate at 145°F until slightly crisp, or smoke at 200°F or less, with several pans of alder wood.

*Hi Mountain Seasonings Alaskan Salmon brine is actually a great choice for all species of fish. This one contains powdered maple syrup for a sweet taste.*

# FISH BRINE 101

- 2–3 pounds fish fillets (salmon, trout, bass, crappie, or most other low-fat freshwater or saltwater species)
- 8 cups water
- 2 cups soy sauce
- 2 cups brown sugar
- ½ cup salt (sea, kosher, or non-iodized)
- 2 tablespoons garlic powder
- 1 tablespoon finely grated ginger or to taste

This is simple homemade brine that cures the fish and leaves the door wide open for you to add your own special spices to taste.

Mix the brine, add the fish, and marinate 12–24 hours or more. Drain, rinse, and allow to air-dry. Add any additional spices or rubs of your choosing and smoke with alder or apple wood, or dehydrate at 145°F until slightly crisp.

*Fish brines from Hi Mountain Seasonings come in three flavors, and each has a slightly different taste. Brines are ready to blend with water, no mixing needed. Bulk bags are also available if you are planning on putting up a large amount of fish for jerking.*

# TANGY SWEET SALMON

- 2 pounds salmon fillets or side (skin on with pin bones removed)
- ½ cup soy sauce
- 2 tablespoons molasses
- 2 tablespoons lemon juice (fresh is better)
- 2 tablespoons ground black pepper
- 1½ teaspoons liquid smoke flavoring

This easy to follow and prepare tangy and sweet salmon jerky recipe comes from the folks at Excalibur Dehydrators (www.excaliburdehydrator.com). Mix all the spices together in a large plastic ziplock bag and blend thoroughly. Marinate for 3 hours . . . or more. We like to brine overnight and up to 24 hours. Then place the fillets in the Excalibur Dehydrator at 130–145°F. Fish will take 12–18 hours until semidry and pliable.

*Kathy Mattoon's grandsons not only love to catch fish and hunt, but they've been turned into avid cooks of all they harvest. Spending a little time with young sportsmen and teaching them how to care for these bounties ensures they will use this life skill and maybe teach their friends.*

# SWEET HAWAIIAN FISH STRIPS OR SHRIMP

- 2 pounds fish fillets (saltwater or freshwater species) or peeled and deveined shrimp
- ½ cup soy sauce
- ½ cup pineapple juice
- 1 cup beer or water
- 1 tablespoon brown sugar
- ¼ teaspoon cayenne pepper
- 1 teaspoon crushed garlic
- 1 teaspoon fresh ginger, minced
- 1 teaspoon salt (sea, kosher, Cajun, non-iodized)
- 1 teaspoon ground black pepper

Mix the brine, add the fish or shrimp, and marinate 12–24 hours or more. Drain, rinse, and allow to air-dry. Add any additional spices or rubs of your choosing, and smoke with alder or apple wood, or dehydrate at 145°F until the fish is slightly crisp, with no wet spots. The shrimp should be dry, but semimoist and bendable.

*Shrimp can always be grilled and BBQed, but if you take them to the next level of drying, they make great seafood jerky. Marinate like fish, add your spices, and leave tail on or off. Smoked on the Traeger Tex with alder wood pellets, we wish we had made more. Store in plastic or vacuum sealed bags. They store great in the refrigerator for a week, or into the freezer until you are ready.*

# WILD CHEFF SMOKED MAPLE

- 5 pounds salmon, lake trout or tuna fillets
- 1 jar Wild Cheff New England Smokehouse Brining Blend (ingredients include California sea salt, hickory smoked sea salt, demerara sugar, green peppercorns, chipotle pepper, garlic, natural mesquite smoke flavor)
- ¾–1 pound light brown sugar
- 1 cup maple syrup

This recipe combines just the right amount of sweet and smoke to produce a unique flavor that may have you referring to it as fish candy. Denny Corriveau is well known and renowned as the *Wild Cheff*. In addition to teaching through television, writing and radio, Corriveau does seminars and teaches wild game and organic cooking through his Free Range Culinary Institute. This recipe comes from him and Wild Cheff Enterprises (www.wildcheff.com) and uses one of their specialty blends of spices. You can always try to duplicate and make a batch of your own, but why? He's been doing it since 1995 and makes it easy with his online offerings of fresh and prepackaged spices.

After mixing fish and brine together, let it marinate 8–12 hours in your refrigerator. Heat your smoker to 200°F with your favorite wood flavors and then smoke the fish between 180–225°F for about six hours. During the drying process, use and brush the fish fillets every 90 minutes with the maple syrup.

*Robby Richardson from Sport Fish Colorado (www.sportfishcolorado.com) hoists a nice lunker. Lake trout, Mackinaw, or lake char can range in size from a few pounds up to around 70 pounds. State records for these fish continue to fall each year. They are a fatty species of fish, but make great jerky with a variety of recipes.*

# CHINESE BBQ FISH BITES

- 2–3 pounds fish fillets
- 2 cups beer or water
- ¼–½ cup hoisin sauce (Chinese BBQ)
- 1 cup soy sauce
- 2–3 tablespoons fish sauce
- 1 teaspoon garlic powder
- 2–3 tablespoons sriracha hot chili or garlic chili sauce

Mix the brine, add the fish, and marinate 12–24 hours or more. Drain, rinse, and allow to air-dry. Add any additional spices or rubs of your choosing, like red pepper flakes, sesame seeds, or an additional basting with the hot or garlic chili sauce. Smoke with alder or apple wood, or dehydrate at 145°F until slightly crisp.

*Stop the drying and smoking process if you want to turn your fish into smoky snacks, or let them continue to dry to a crispy texture for jerky. In the Camp Chef wood pellet stove/grill, you can greatly increase the drying space with their jerky rack insert.*

# LOBSTER LUMPS

- 3–4 or more live Maine lobsters
- ½ cup lemon pepper
- 1 can dark beer
- 1–2 tablespoons lemon juice (fresh or bottled)
- 2–3 tablespoons favorite hot sauce to taste (optional)

Use this recipe when you really want to impress the family and your friends with lobster jerky! Recipe and lobsters come from Ellen and Mike Albert at A&A Hardware & Lobster Company (www.aalobster.com) in Greene, Maine. They not only ship around the country, but can even make special arrangements to have fresh live Maine lobsters delivered to your camp on the next outdoor adventure.

Boil, bake, or grill the whole lobster as if you were preparing it for the dinner table. That way you can "crack everything" and get all the meat from the tail and claws. You'll probably want to order an extra lobster or two so that all the cooked lobster meat doesn't disappear before getting a chance to be made into jerky!

Mix cooked lobster meat chunks/slices and marinade together in plastic bag/container and allow to overnight marinate in your refrigerator.

Drain marinade, but do not rinse. Place lobster slices/chunks on a nonstick sprayed cookie sheet and gently dry in your home oven at 200°F. Lobster meat is very delicate, and you'll need to keep your eyes on it so that it does not overcook and turn rubbery. Start checking the meat after about 90 minutes. You can also drizzle a little more lemon juice and sprinkle more lemon pepper on the meat as it dries for more flavoring.

*Baked, boiled, or broiled, live Maine lobsters are a real treat. Especially if you can have A&A Lobster Company fly them in and have them delivered to your camp! Lobster is also easy to dehydrate or smoke into great jerky. Just make sure your friends are deserving of such a special delicacy.*

# CHAPTER 13
# WINGING IT WITH POULTRY JERKY

When working with poultry, especially store-bought turkey or chicken, heed the same words of caution about finished meat temperature as you would with pork, bear, and other critters: All of these meats are safest to eat as jerky once the internal meat temperature has reached 160°F. Below that, and there is a chance that it is not safe. If you are using an oven or smoker, it's pretty easy to get the meat temp up to that safe level. If you are using a dehydrator and your unit does not heat and dry at 160–165°F, you may want to precook the meat strips by boiling (5–10 minutes) or baking (30–40 minutes) before you marinate/cure the meats and prepare them for the dehydrator.

We've used wild poultry, game birds, waterfowl, and store-bought chickens and turkey . . . and have never (willingly) had to precook any of the meats. We've one it for our recipe testing, and while it had a good flavor profile, the chicken and turkey meats definitely had a different meat texture. It is however an option you may want to use.

Like all meat strips and ground meat snacks, marinating/brining the poultry for 12–24 hours will bring out the fullest of flavors. Or you can accelerate that marination and infusing process by using vacuum canisters that often come with vacuum sealers, or the Marinade Express appliance that vacuums and tumbles the meat and marinades together.

*The Texas Pro from Traeger Wood Pellet Grills is one of the large, heavy-duty dual-use BBQ grills and smokers. Electric auto ignition system and a large wood pellet reservoir will keep your meats smoking at just the right temperature from start to finish. Our marinated and spiced mountain lion meat strips took about two hours with the temperature set at 200°F.*

# HI MOUNTAIN POULTRY BRINE

- 5–10 pounds whole or pieced poultry (any species)
- 1 pouch Hi Mountain Seasonings poultry brine for each gallon of water
- 1 gallon of chilled water

Hi Mountain Seasonings (www.himtnjerky.com) makes *Brown Sugar brine* mix, and their long-standing *Game Bird & Poultry brine* blend. Both are easy to use if you do not want or have the time to make your own brine from scratch. And while brining is not always required with poultry, it does offer an additional layer of flavor by adding salt and sweetness to the meat.

Once the brine is mixed, place the birds or cut pieces/fillets into the brine so that they are totally immersed, and refrigerate/brine for 24 hours or more. Once brined, wash the birds and allow to air-dry. Take off all the skin, and cut the meats into strips about ¼- to ⅜-inch thick. Here is where you can now leave the poultry meat strips alone and ready them for the smoker/dehydrator, or add your own mix of spices/rubs. Some of our favorite "add on" spices include Cajun and regular seasoning salt, ground or red pepper flakes, lemon pepper, hot sauce (your favorite), and brown sugar. If you want to go exotic and really impress your friends, you might want to find a bottle of cHarissa (www.charissaspice.com), which is an authentic Moroccan spice rub that is a combination of cumin, paprika, garlic powder, cayenne pepper, and sea salt. It makes the jerky taste like nothing you have likely ever tried and you will love it!

Dehydrate at 155–165°F until slightly crisp but bendable. Or smoke at 175–200°F with several pans of apple wood.

*Hi Mountain Seasonings has a few jerky cures that are designed specifically for turkey and waterfowl. However, don't be afraid to use some of their other blends for poultry as well. Their Inferno Blend and Mesquite mix for wild goose also worked well on the turkey jerky.*

# ROSEMARY TANGY LEMON

- 2 pounds turkey/chicken meat strips (breasts or thigh meat)
- ⅓–½ can of beer or 6 ounces of water
- 3 tablespoons lemon juice
- 1½ tablespoons rosemary
- 2 tablespoons lemon pepper spice
- 1 teaspoon garlic powder or fresh crushed garlic

Simple and flavorful, the rosemary and the lemon pepper combine together for a savory jerky strip. Can be oven-dried, dehydrated, or smoked.

*The comeback and proliferation of wild turkeys throughout many states makes it a favorite for spring and fall hunters. Big toms (males) can tip the scales from 16-24 pounds. That's a lot of great turkey jerky waiting for the smoker, oven, or dehydrator. Photo courtesy of the Utah Division of Wildlife Resources.*

# EXCALIBUR'S SPICY TURKEY

- 2 pounds sliced turkey meat (thighs or breasts)
- ¾ cup soy sauce
- 3 tablespoons honey
- 2 tablespoons chili-garlic paste
- 2 teaspoons red chili flakes or to taste

If you want to spice up your bird and enjoy good heat and great flavor, this recipe from the folks at Excalibur Dehydrators (www.excaliburdehydrator.com) is a pretty good choice for pepper bellies!

Skin the birds and cut into ¼- to ⅜-inch thick strips. Marinate 12–24 hours and dehydrate at 155–165°F until the strips bend and are crisp, but don't snap and break.

*Authors Kathy and Andy will make turkey jerky with a bird from the grocery store if they have to, but much prefer to head for the hills and harvest their own. Even big tough toms become tender once marinated and dehydrated or smoked.*

# HELLISH HABANERO APPLE

- 2 pounds turkey, chicken, game birds or waterfowl breast strips
- 3–5 habanero chilies, chopped
- 2 teaspoons crushed/diced garlic
- 1½ tablespoons fresh ginger root, chopped
- 1½ tablespoons curing salt
- ½ cup applesauce
- 1 cup apple juice
- ½ cup apple cider vinegar
- ½ cup beer or water
- 4 tablespoons lemon juice (fresh or bottled)
- ½ cup brown sugar
- ½ cup white sugar

If you like lots of heat and flavor and want to work up a sweat without ever moving away from the smoke or dehydrator, this apple-flavored habanero is sure to "light up your life!" Worst part of the preparation for this recipe is that once everything for the marinade is mixed together in a saucepan, it needs to be heated and stirred so that the sugars melt completely. We suggest that you do this in a well ventilated or on an outdoor stove. *Otherwise the fumes will be choking, guaranteed!*

Once boiled for a few minutes, allow the volcano mixture to cool before transferring it to a blender or food processor. Puree thoroughly, add meat and liquid to plastic bag/container, and marinate 12–24 hours. This recipe also works well with the Marinade Express vacuum/tumbler or with vacuum canister systems with vacuum sealers.

Wear gloves when removing meat for the dehydrator, oven, or smoker. The marinade is insanely hot and will burn your lips, eyes, nose, and other body parts it comes in contact with. Dehydrate at 155–165°F; oven-dry at 175–200°F; or dry in the smoker at 200°F with apple or alder wood.

*Turkey, like chicken, needs to be cut, sliced and processed for seasoning by itself to avoid cross contamination with any other foods. Make sure when finished slicing that cutlery, cutting board, the entire area, and your hands get washed and disinfected.*

# CRANAPPLE CHICKEN

- 2 pounds chicken, game birds, turkey or waterfowl breast strips
- 2 cups white cranberry-apple or white cranberry-peach juice
- 1½ tablespoons curing salt
- 2 tablespoons black pepper
- 1 can dark beer or 1½ cups of water
- 3 tablespoons soy sauce
- 1 teaspoon cayenne pepper
- 1 teaspoon onion powder
- 1 teaspoon poultry seasoning
- 1 teaspoon liquid smoke flavoring (optional)

This is a sweet cranberry and apple flavor combination that works universally well on all types of poultry. As you can see, it is simply sweet with no heat!

If you are going to oven-dry (200°F) or dehydrate, add the liquid smoke flavoring for an additional taste. If you are going to smoke it, apple or mesquite are good wood flavor choices. You'll know the jerky is done when they are dry, but fairly bendable and tender. Over drying them will make them brittle and tough to chew. If you are using an oven, check on them after 90 minutes. If you're using a deyhdrator, start checking after 5–6 hours, and if you're using a smoker, start checking after 2 hours.

*Dove breasts, like duck and geese, are dark and flavorful. Slice the meat chunks from the breastbone, marinate and dry on the Coleman NXT propane grill. You can keep the temperature low (under 200°F) by simply igniting only one burner and keeping your jerky as far away from the heat as possible.*

# TERIYAKI GARLIC

- 2 pounds waterfowl, chicken, game birds, or turkey strips
- 1 cup teriyaki sauce
- 1 cup beer or water
- 1 cup sake (optional)
- 1 tablespoon minced garlic or garlic powder
- ½ teaspoon Cajun salt
- ½ teaspoon freshly ground black pepper
- ½–1 teaspoon red pepper flakes
- ½ teaspoon liquid smoke flavoring (optional)
- 1½ teaspoons curing salt

Duck and goose breast strips (dark meat) are a favorite for this recipe, but you can use turkey, chicken, and any game bird as well. If you are going to oven-dry (175–200°F) or dehydrate (155–165°F) you might want to add the liquid smoke flavoring. If you are going to put it in the smoker, apple and alder woods are the top choices.

*Duck breast meat can be cut into great jerky strips. The meat is dark and flavorful, and is also a great choice for grinding and making into snackin' sticks.*

# SPICY GOOSE JERKY

- 2 pounds goose or duck strips
- 1½ tablespoons curing salt
- 1 cup brown sugar
- 1 cup water
- ¾ cup soy sauce
- ½ cup Worcestershire sauce
- 2 tablespoons garlic powder
- 2 tablespoons chili powder
- 3 tablespoons coarsely ground black pepper
- 2 tablespoons red pepper flakes

A spicy, tried-and-true recipe from the folks at Ducks Unlimited (www.ducks.org) that works great with both goose and duck meat. Marinate for 24 hours and meats can be oven-dried (200°F), dehydrated, or dried in the smoker with apple wood for a sweeter flavor. If you want to go bold, use mesquite, cherry, or hickory.

*Snow geese, like wild hogs, are becoming overpopulated in many states, and are a great resource for hunters with open bag limits and extended hunting seasons. Like all waterfowl, they make great jerky snacks. Just trim off any fat from around the breast meat. Photo courtesy of the Utah Division of Wildlife Resources.*

# EVERYDAY POULTRY MARINADE

- 2 pounds poultry strips—turkey, chicken, waterfowl
- ¼ cup each lemon juice
- ¼ cup balsamic vinegar
- ¼ cup honey
- 1 cup dry red wine
- ½ cup soy sauce
- 3 tablespoons minced garlic
- 3 tablespoons fresh rosemary leaves, minced
- 2 tablespoons Dijon mustard
- 2 teaspoons black pepper
- ½ teaspoon red pepper flakes

This is a recipe from Marinade Express (www.marinadeexpress.com) that is sweet heat, tangy, and savory all at the same time! We left out the olive oil in their original recipe because instead of heading to the grill with our meat, we wanted to smoke it up with apple wood.

With all ingredients mixed together, you can marinate the meat strips for 12–24 hours in your refrigerator, or if you have a Marinade Express (vacuum/tumbler) system, the ingredients and the meat are put into the vacuum canister where all the air is vacuumed out in about 5 minutes. Then you use the tumbler system and give everything a spin for about 30 minutes. After that, you're ready to lay the meat strips out on the jerky racks and begin smoking. The entire marinating/infusion process takes less than an hour instead of a full day!

*Steve McGrath from Camp Chef Products took some of his Maine sea ducks and turned them into jerky strips for everyone in our hunting camp. Guess what he used? The Camp Chef Smoke Vault.*

# RED WINE & WORCESTERSHIRE WATERFOWL

- 2–3 pounds poultry strips—duck and goose work best
- 2 cups dry red wine or unsweetened cranberry juice
- 1 cup fruit juice—apple, orange, or pineapple
- 1 cup Worcestershire sauce
- ¼–⅓ cup Cajun seasoning salt, or to taste
- 1 tablespoon garlic powder

This recipe came from one of the grandsons of a family that has become worldwide famous for their Cajun seasonings. It is one that will make a convert out of anyone that believes that duck or goose is strong and gamey tasting. *Friends that take a courtesy bite always come back and ask for more.* Using different fruit juice flavors give the meats a lot of different profiles, so make sure you try them all.

Mix all the spices and liquids together in with the waterfowl strips and marinate for 24+ hours. Drain and load up the smoker racks with apple wood. Heat/dry at around 200°F. With this recipe, many like it when the meat is still soft, very pliable, and not cooked much more than medium rare. The meat's shelf life won't be very long unless sealed and frozen . . . but around here, we've rarely had any leftovers to worry about!

*Everyone knows that corn-fed mallards make delicious jerky. But virtually all waterfowl, including the "off species" like snow geese and diver ducks, are also great. The authors suggest you trim off the fat and you will eliminate any fishy flavor.*

# HAPPY, HAPPY, HAPPY BIRD JERKY

- 2–3 pounds poultry strips—duck, goose, chicken, turkey, or any favorite game bird
- ½ cup beer or water
- 1 cup bourbon or brandy (not optional)
- ¼ cup teriyaki sauce
- ¼ cup soy sauce
- 1 tablespoon liquid smoke flavoring (hickory)
- 2–3 tablespoons Cajun seasoning salt
- 3–4 tablespoons Louisiana hot sauce to taste

We got this recipe years ago while duck hunting down in the back bayous of Louisiana, and it's been a favorite for anyone that loves poultry jerky with a bold bourbon or brandy flavor. Marinate the meat strips for 24+ hours in your refrigerator. Drain and allow to air-dry; put the strips on the dehydrator trays at 155–165°F till the strips crisp up but are not overly chewy. Can also be smoked with apple wood at 200°F.

*It doesn't get much prettier than this, with wild pheasants busting out of cornfields and on the fly. Pheasants have flavorful white-meat breasts that can be smoked or dried into great jerky.*

# CHAPTER 14
# PORK, BEAR, AND WILD CRITTERS

This is one of those recipe sections where a variety of meats are going to be lumped together. The reason is that domestic pork, wild hog, bear, beaver, raccoon, marmot, rabbit, and others come with a word of caution. According to all the health/science folks, all of these meats are safest to eat as jerky once the internal meat temperature has reached 160°F. Below that, there is a chance that it is not safe. If you are using an oven or smoker, it's pretty easy to get the meat temp up to that safe level. If you are using a dehydrator and your unit does not heat and dry at 160–165°F, you may want to precook the meat strips by boiling (5–10 minutes) or by baking (30–40 minutes) before you marinate/cure the meats and prepare them for the dehydrator.

This rule however does not apply to *bacon!* If you are planning on making dried, smoked, or oven-baked commercial bacon, you do NOT have to precook the slices. Just make sure that the bacon cooks thoroughly and is nice and crisp!

As with all our other recipes, many of these can be further enhanced with beer, wine, tequila, bourbon, rum, Grand Marnier, etc. *The alcohol evaporates out, but the flavor stays with the meats!*

Make sure that your dehydrator trays and jerky racks are well coated with oil or a nonstick spray.

*Photo by Lynn Chamberlain, Utah Division of Wildlife Resources.*

# HI MOUNTAIN JERKY STRIPS

- 2 pounds lean pork meat strips or other game meat strips
- 1 tablespoon + 2 teaspoons Hi Mountain Seasonings
- 1 tablespoon + 2 teaspoons Hi Mountain Cure

Of all the "ready to use" commercial jerky making rubs and cures that are available on the marketplace today, you'd be hard-pressed to find better quality and flavor selection than those from Hi Mountain Seasonings (www.himtnjerky.com). While we have dozens of recipes for making your jerky and meat sticks from scratch and home ingredients, sometimes you simply want to take the easy way to make great snacks. With eighteen different Hi Mountain jerky flavors, they are ready to roll out of the box, or can be modified and added to for your custom flavors—garlic or onion powder, ground black/red pepper, and more.

You can precook (boil or bake) the pork, bear, or other types of meat strips if you want to, before starting the curing process.

Take the meat strips and place into a plastic bag or container. Add the cure and seasonings to the meat, and let marinate/cure in your refrigerator for 12–24 hours or more. This is a dry cure/seasoning mix, so no additional liquid is required.

*Hi Mountain Seasonings's Bourbon BBQ jerky cure is great by itself, or you can add a little more sweetness with your own brown sugar. We kicked up the heat and topped the bison strips off with some red pepper flakes.*

# SWEET AND SOUR PORK/GAME STRIPS

- 2 pounds lean pork meat strips (works also with bear, marmot, beaver, coon, etc.)
- 2 tablespoons hoisin (Chinese BBQ sauce)
- 1 cup beer or water
- 1 cup pineapple juice
- 2 tablespoons soy sauce
- ½ cup rice wine or red wine vinegar
- 2–3 teaspoons lemon juice (fresh or bottled)
- ⅓ cup brown sugar
- 1 teaspoon onion powder
- 1–2 teaspoons garlic salt
- 1½ tablespoons curing salt
- 3–4 drops of red food coloring (optional)

If you love the taste of smothered sweet & sour pork bites at your favorite Chinese restaurant, you're going to want to make this pork (or other game) jerky recipe one of your favorites!

Mix all liquid and spice ingredients in a pan, then heat on the stove top until brown sugar is melted in. Adding a few drops of red food coloring will give the meat that traditional reddish color like you see in the restaurants. You can add more beer or water if you plan to precook/boil the meat. If not, let the liquid cool to room temperature, then add the meat strips and marinate in the refrigerator for 12–24 hours. This recipe is great for the dehydrator, or can be dried in your oven at 170–200°F.

*Wild hogs in many states have become extremely overpopulated and are more than just destructive pests. Damage from large herds of hogs can be catastrophic to ranchers, farmers, and other native wildlife. On the plus side, they are relatively easy to hunt, and make fantastic jerky and ground meat snacks. Photo courtesy of Remington Firearms.*

# HONEY GLAZED PORK/GAME BITES

- 2 pounds ground pork or other game meat
- 4 tablespoons soy sauce
- 2 tablespoons fish sauce
- 2 tablespoons sherry or sweet wine (red or white)
- 2 tablespoons honey
- ½ teaspoon ground black pepper
- 1 teaspoon Chinese five-spice powder
- 2 tablespoons sugar
- 2 teaspoons curing salt (optional)
- ½–1 teaspoon ground red/cayenne pepper to taste
- 1 tablespoon roasted sesame seeds (optional)
- ½ cup additional honey and sherry/sweet wine to taste for basting

We picked this recipe up about forty years ago from one of Andy's college roommates that was from Hong Kong. He says that this recipe had been in his family for generations and was made for special family holidays. *Forget that! It's great year-round and is ideal for the home oven or smoker.* It is also a recipe where you do not have to precook any of the meats.

Mix the meat and spices in a bowl thoroughly and then marinate in the refrigerator for 4–24 hours. Squish flat on a cookie sheet and cut into small bites, or use your jerky gun and make rounds or strips.

This is a fast, high-heat cook/dry recipe instead of low and slow. Heat the oven or smoker to 375°F and spray the jerky rack or pan with nonstick oil. Cook/smoke for about 10–12 minutes, baste with the honey/wine mixture, and turn the strips or rounds over. Cook/smoke for another 5 minutes, then baste again. Continue this process till meat is semidry and until the honey/wine basting mix has added a nice caramel color.

Around here, we can never seem to make enough of the pork bites, so using the curing salt is only necessary if you are going to seal it freeze it. If left in the refrigerator, use the curing salt and it will last up to a month or more.

*Yellow-bellied marmots and other common woodchucks and rockchucks make some surprisingly great jerky! Trim off all the animal's fat and process it like pork meat. Photo courtesy of the Utah Division of Wildlife Resources.*

# MANGO HABANERO STRIPS

- 1 pound lean meat pork strips
- 1 cup mango juice
- ½ cup brown sugar
- 1–1½ tablespoons curing salt
- 1 can of beer
- ¼ cup tequila (optional)
- 1–3 finely diced habanero peppers (to your heat levels)

Pretty simple, straightforward, and HOT! Mix together ingredients and marinate the meat strips from 12–24 hours and oven dry at 200°F for about 2+ hours or until meat temperature is above 160°F and the strips are dry but pliable. For the smoker, just about any and all of your favorite wood flavor types will give the porky strips a smoky BBQ taste and experience. Be warned: Habanero peppers are a lot hotter than any jalapeño, so start out easy and build to your tolerance or inferno level!

*Wild hogs are considered rampant and destructive in many states, and it is only going to get worse. That's good news for hunters because the pork meats can all be processed into ground meat snackin' sticks or great tasting jerky strips. Oven-dried, in the dehydrator, or best of all . . . in the smoker, just make sure the internal meat temperature reaches 160°F.*

# CANDIED BACON STRIPS

- 1 pound smoked/sliced bacon (*you'll wish you made more*)
- ½ cup brown sugar
- ½–1 teaspoon ground red/cayenne pepper—to taste
- 1 tablespoon red pepper flakes (to garnish)

As everyone knows, the world is a much better place in which to live, thanks to bacon! This takes oven-baked bacon up a couple of notches in the flavor department and turns it into a sweet treat. Try making 1 pound, and you'll wish you made 3 or 4 pounds!

Mix sugar and red/cayenne pepper well in a bowl. Coat/dip each strip of bacon thoroughly with the mixture and lay out on a metal jerky rack onto of a baking pan/ cookie sheet. This way the bacon grease will drip away from the strips and into the pan. Preheat the oven to 225°F and plan on cooking/drying for about 1 hour before turning bacon over. Cook for 1 more hour or until the bacon is crisp. Garnish/sprinkle with additional red pepper flakes if you want a little more heat.

*Making bacon into jerky is about as simple as adding your favorite spices/flavors and then oven baking slowly. Both turkey and pork bacon work well. For heat—try basting with hot sauce. For savory—try lemon pepper. For sweet—brown sugar or maple syrup.*

# RATTLIN' AND SIZZLIN' SNACK BITES

- 1 or 2 large rattlesnakes, deboned meat (2–3 cups)
- 1 cup rice vinegar (mild) or balsamic vinegar (bold)
- 4–6 tablespoons bourbon
- 1 tablespoon curing salt
- 2 tablespoons Hi Mountain Seasonings's Soy Ginger Marinade or your favorite dry spice marinade

We've eaten a lot of different snake species from around the world, and it's pretty darn good when fried or baked and then all seasoned up. *And no, it doesn't taste like chicken,* it tastes like snake, and that's a good mild and sweet meat. We've also learned over the years that snake can be smoked/dried and turned into delicious jerky.

If there's a ten-foot rattler or giant anaconda on the menu, you'll have plenty of snake bite chucks. Skinny snakes (regardless of species) are simply too much trouble to debone and get the meat bites. Bigger snakes, however, skin and fillet pretty well by using your knife to follow down the backbone and around the long, long, long ribcage.

Snake is a white and light colored meat that can be prepared much like poultry. Mix your meat chunks and marinade together and let it sit 12–24 hours. Remove meat and drain, and spread it out on your smoker's jerky racks. Keep the smoker's temperature at less than 200°F and use sweet woods like alder or apple for smoking. Meat should be dry and firm, but not overcooked to be rubbery and chewy.

*He's probably not real happy knowing he's going to be turned into jerky, but snakes such as this Great Basin rattlesnake in southwestern Utah make great eats. Photo by Lynn Chamberlain, Utah Division of Wildlife Resources.*

# CHAPTER 15

# DRIED FRUITS

Everyone knows that most fruits are seasonal. This means that if you want certain fresh fruits on a year-round basis, you are going to pay a fortune for them. *Bummer!* Take a stroll over to the grocery section where you can find the *"dried fruits"* and you are guaranteed to go into sticker shock when you see that those little packages are selling for!

Instead of having to make a major investment, it's easy to either dehydrate or sometimes even put a smoky flavor onto those fruits that you can turn into year-round snacks by drying, bagging, and freezing.

Once again, all you have to do is get creative with your recipes. Some of our recipes are "ripe and ready" for experimentation with a splash of bourbon, sweet or dry wines, tequila, rum, or a favorite flavored liquor.

Most fruits can be peeled if desired, and one peeling trick is to immerse the whole fruits in boiling water for about thirty seconds, then *shock* them in an ice water bath. The skins on everything from apples, peaches, nectarines, blueberries, and apricots will come off easily. Or you can leave the fruit slices with the skin on and go *natural*.

Fresh fruits when dried often have a tendency to discolor and darken. There is nothing wrong with this, but some of that can be treated with a water soaking mix of ascorbic acid (found in the spice section at the grocery store). Usually a 30–60 minute soak is all that's needed. Or you can add simply add a couple of teaspoons of lemon or lime juice to the fruits. Some of our recipes call for orange, pineapple, and other *acidic* juices, so that's another way to avoid discoloring.

Make sure that you oil or spray a nonstick cooking spray on all your dehydrator and smoking racks. Fruits, because of their high sugar content, will stick if you don't.

Dehydrating fruit seems to work best at from 135–145°F. Fruits can be semi-pliable to bone dry, depending upon your preference and tastes. Drying times will vary greatly depending upon outside or inside temperature and humidity. Use the dehydrator maker's guide as a reference.

*Mangoes make great dehydrated fruit snacks. Pitted and skinned, the fruit slices are naturally sweet and tangy. Dip the slices in a little honey and lemon juice, and that's all you need to do before drying.*

Because fruits really do need low-temperature drying, if you are going to add a little smoke to them, make sure you closely monitor your smoker's internal temperature. If you have a cold smoke system, you can add a little smoke in a variety of flavors without adding any heat. Once a *touch of smoke* has been added, simply transfer the fruits back to your dehydrator and finish them off!

Once dried, and if the humidity levels are low, it is best to let the fruit air-dry for 8–10 hours before bagging or vacuum sealing. Dried fruits can be stored in your refrigerator for weeks, or months and months if put in the freezer.

## TANGY BANANAS

- 1 large bunch of bananas—7–10 total
- 2–3 cups pineapple, mango, or orange juice
- ½ cup honey (optional)
- ⅓ cup brandy (optional)
- ¼ cup cinnamon and sugar mix/blend (optional)

Dried, store-bought banana chips are expensive and most come with a coating of corn syrup that can add a ton of calories. With these banana chips, you can keep it easy by simply slicing the bananas either lengthwise or crosscut into ⅜-inch strips and oven-dry or dehydrate. Ripe, even overripe, bananas are going to be sweeter and have more flavor.

Taking it up a notch in the flavor department; try marinating the banana slices in pineapple, mango, or orange juice in a plastic bag/container in the refrigerator for 2–4 hours. Adding honey and brandy are a nice touch as well. Remove from the juice and add a couple more drops of honey or sprinkle on a mix of ground cinnamon/sugar. Dry/dehydrate until crisp at 135°F.

*Bananas can be finished off for the dehydrator by adding a sprinkle of sugar/cinnamon or simply dipping them in honey. Chips with the honey will take a little longer to dry and are going to be sticky but delicious.*

# NUTMEG APRICOTS

- 2–3 pounds ripe apricots (peeled or unpeeled)
- 1–2 cups fruit juice
- ¼ cup sugar
- 1–2 tablespoons ground nutmeg to taste

Pit/core your apricots and slice into quarters or eighths, depending upon the size of the fruit. Apricots have a tendency to discolor and turn brown when dehydrated, so you can bathe the fruit in a quart of water with ½ teaspoon of ascorbic acid or powdered vitamin C for an hour in a plastic bag/container inside your refrigerator. Or you can use a couple of cups of fruit juice—orange, pineapple, apple, mango, or even cranberry!

Remove from the liquid, and lightly dust the slices with the sugar and the ground nutmeg. Apricots are best dried in a dehydrator at around 135–140°F. until they are soft and bendable. Let air-dry for 8–10 hours before plastic bag or vacuum sealing.

*Fresh fruits not readily available? No problem! Many canned fruit favorites can be drained and dried with great results. Pineapple, peaches, apricots, nectarines, and pears are the top favorites.*

# CRUNCHY BERRIES, GRAPES, AND CHERRIES

- 2–6 cups berries (blue, black, raspberry), grapes, or cherries
- 1–2 cups sweet red or white wine or apple juice
- ⅛–¼ cup powdered sugar

Dried berries, grapes, cherries, or whatever "sweet" favorite is available make a great snack on their own or as a bonus flavor for your trail mix for backcountry eating. Once dried, they can also be used in your pancakes, cookies, cakes, or morning breakfast cereal.

Cherries have to be pitted, but the others do not. Pretreatment isn't mandatory, but blueberries have a tough skin that can be "cracked" by dipping them in boiling water for about 30 seconds, and then into an ice bath for about 30 seconds.

Add a cup or two of sweet wine or apple juice to the berries, grapes, or cherries and let them marinate in your refrigerator for 2–6 hours. Remove from the liquid and lightly dust them with powdered sugar. Fruits are best dehydrated at 135–145°F until they shrivel and become dry. They can be oven-dried if you are careful to keep the temperature below 200°F by cracking the oven door and keeping a watchful eye on the fruit. Once dried, you may want to add a little more powdered sugar dusting.

*Some might call them raisins, but homemade dehydrated or smoked grapes (apple or cherry wood) are not going to taste like anything you've ever had that comes out of a box from the grocery store.*

# ORANGEY CRAN APPLES

- 3–5 pounds of your favorite tart and tangy apples (peeled or unpeeled)
- 3–4 cups orange juice
- 3–4 cups cranberry juice
- ¼ cup Hot Damn! liquor or Apple Pucker schnapps (optional)
- 1 cup cinnamon/sugar mix (optional)

Smoked or dehydrated apples are one of the easiest of all the fruits to prepare and enjoy, either as a trail snack or for your morning cereal or granola mix. Just select apples that are firm, tangy, and tart, like Granny Smith. Gala, Red/Golden Delicious, Fuji, and other "sweet" apples often turn mushy when dried or smoked.

Core your apples, and peel them if that is your preference. Cut into ¼-inch slices and mix in plastic bag/container with orange juice and cranberry juice. Do not mix in the sugar/cinnamon, as this is an "after drying" garnish. Add the Hot Damn! or Apple Pucker liquor to the mix for a real boost in flavor. Let them marinate in the refrigerator for 4–6 hours. Remove from liquid and they are ready to dry or smoke, or sprinkle lightly with the cinnamon/sugar mix. While dehydrating is easy at 135°F until crisp, you can actually add a smoky flavor with your gas or electric smoker. Keep the temperature at 175°F or less and add a pan or two of apple or alder wood for a nice woodsy touch. Apples are also ideal for using cold smoke.

*Select apples for the dehydrator or smoker that are crisp and have a tangy flavor. Skin on or peeled, apples can be spiced up with a sugar/cinnamon mix, or you can go a little "wild," with mixes of nutmeg, allspice, ground cloves, or even pumpkin pie spice!*

# BOURBON PEARS

- 3–5 pounds of ripe pears—Anjou, Bartlett, Bosc, or Forelle
- 2–3 cups bourbon
- 2–3 cups fruit juice—apple, orange, or pineapple
- 1 tablespoon cayenne/red pepper—ground or flakes
- ½–1 tablespoon salt (sea, kosher, or non-iodized)

This is a New Orleans flavor twist that beats the heck out of simply coring and drying pears in your smoker or dehydrator. The pears are super sweet with the fruit juice, and the bourbon adds an earthy taste while the ground/flaked pepper adds a little zip!

Put your ¼-inch slices (skin on) in a plastic bag/container with the bourbon, fruit juice, and salt and red pepper, and let it marinate in the refrigerator 4–6 hours or overnight. Remove slices from the liquid; you can add a little additional pepper sprinkles for more kick. The slices can be dehydrated at around 140°F till semidry and bendable. They can also be cold smoked, or placed in your smoker with a couple of pans of apple, alder, or cherry wood on low temperature. Let the pears air-dry before bagging them up.

# PEPPERY MANGO PEACHES

- 3–5 pounds ripe peaches (peeled or unpeeled)
- ½ cup ground black pepper
- 2–3 cups mango juice
- ½ to 1 tablespoon salt (sea, kosher, or non-iodized)

If you like the taste of black pepper on your fruit, as compared to the heat from ground cayenne, red pepper, chipotle, or habanero, this is a great way to increase the peaches, flavor profile.

After pitting the peaches, cut them into ¼-inch slices, add the mango juice, and put everything into a plastic bag or container and let marinate in the refrigerator for a few hours. Remove the fruit from the liquid, and toss the slices gently in a bowl with the salt and ground black pepper to taste.

Dehydrate until semi-crisp or crispy at around 135–140°F. Leave the peaches to air-dry overnight before plastic bagging or vacuum sealing.

*Preparing baskets full of fresh peaches requires simply removing the pit and slicing for the dehydrator. They can be quick-boiled and ice-water shocked if you want to remove the skins.*

# SWEET PINEAPPLE KIWI

- 1–2 pounds ripe kiwi, peeled
- ½–1 teaspoon salt (sea, kosher, or non-iodized)
- 1–2 cups pineapple juice
- 3 tablespoons powdered sugar (optional)

Kiwifruit may not be at the top of your list of dried snacks, but it is certainly one worth pursuing with your dehydrator. Once dried, the sweetness of the fruit is condensed, and the addition of a little salt and pineapple juice adds to a great tropical dried and munchy morsel.

After peeling the kiwi skin, simply slice the fruit into ¼-inch slivers. Marinate in the salt and pineapple juice for 4–6 hours in your refrigerator inside a plastic bag or container. Dry in the dehydrator at 135°F until dry and bendable. Sometimes the kiwi has a "tang" to it, so you may want to sprinkle/dust the fruit with a little powdered sugar before drying.

*Ripe kiwifruits make tangy chips when dried. Peel off skin, slice about ¼-inch thick, and place on nonstick sprayed dehydrator tray. They can be soft and bendable, or dried up crispy.*

# SOUTH OF THE BORDER STRAWBERRIES

- 2–3 pounds fresh, ripe strawberries
- 1 cup orange or apple juice
- 1 cup dark tequila or mescal (not optional)
- ½–1 teaspoon salt (sea, kosher, or non-iodized) or Cajun salt

Whether you've eaten them in breakfast cereal, granola, oatmeal, packages, or just munched handfuls of them at home or on the trail, dried strawberries are hard to beat! As with all the recipes that call for booze, the alcohol cooks out of the foods, and it is used as a flavor-enhancer only. With the tequila and the fruit juice flavoring, these give the strawberries a sweet and full flavor. The salt helps balance that, and the Cajun salt/spice adds a little zing.

After stemming the strawberries, slice them in half and marinate in the tequila/mescal, fruit juice, and the salt or Cajun salt for a few hours in your refrigerator in a plastic bag or container. Strawberries cut into halves or sliced can be dried in your home oven if you can keep the temperatures 150–170°F. Try propping the oven door open with a wood spoon. If headed for the dehydrator, ideal is 135–145°F.

*Strawberries once dried in the dehydrator go great with your Chex Mix or other trail snack and nut mixtures. Once stemmed, strawberries are cut in half. Adding sugar to sweeten them up is optional.*

# TANGY HONEY MANGO

- 4–6 mango fruits (pitted, peeled, and sliced)
- ¼ cup lemon juice
- 2 tablespoons honey

Mangoes, of which there are over 2,000 varieties, have been grown and harvested here in the U.S. since the 1880s. Today it rates as one of the most cultivated fruits in the world. In spite of it having a giant "pit" that can be a challenge to remove, this fruit dries well and retains a lot of natural flavor. It's also a favorite for drying because in most areas around the country, it's available on a year-round basis.

After pitting and peeling, slice the mangoes into small ⅜-inch strips. Mix honey and lemon juice in a bowl, and microwave the concoction for about 30 seconds so that the honey melts slightly and blends with lemon juice. Dip the mango fruit strips into the liquid and dehydrate at 135°F, until the fruit is semidry and leathery. Use the leftover honey/mango liquid for basting while the fruit dries.

*Mango fruit strips topped off with a little salt and some ground cinnamon and a splash of fresh-squeezed lemon is great trail snack. Use a potato/veggie peeler to strip the skin and a sharp knife to remove the pit. They're delicious dehydrated or lightly smoked with apple wood.*

# MELONS GONE MAD!

- 2 ripe cantaloupe melons (rind and seeds removed and sliced)
- 1 medium or large watermelon (rind removed and sliced)
- Sea salt to taste

Fresh melons are a summer favorite for everyone. However, taking cantaloupe and watermelon and turning them into super sweet candy is as simple as removing the rind and slicing the inside fruit to whatever length pleases you. Add a few sprinkles of sea salt, and let the melon meats dry to a leather consistency in your dehydrator at 135°F.

*Cantaloupes in camp are great fruits and snacks; however, they are heavy and bruise easily. Peeled, seeded and sliced for the dehydrator, they make lightweight and sweet trail treats. Just sprinkle with some sea salt for flavoring and dry them up! Photo courtesy of USDA.*

# DROP DEAD SIMPLE PINEAPPLE

- 1–2 large fresh pineapples (skinned, cored, and sliced) or 1–2 cans of sliced pineapple)
- 1–2 teaspoons salt (sea, kosher, or non-iodized)

Pineapples from Hawaii are nearly a year-round staple at most large grocery stores. However, packing one into camp on your outdoor adventures is bulky and cumbersome. Turning it into a great dried snack treat is as easy as cutting off both ends, trimming off the prickly skin, taking out the core, and slicing it into long, ½-inch-thick slices. Or you can use 1–2 cans of sliced pineapple, drained.

Pineapple dries extremely well in a dehydrator at 135°F and is ready to remove when it bends gently without breaking or snapping. Your finished sticks are going to be sweet, chewy, and slightly sticky. Cut up into small chunks, it's an ideal addition to your trail mixes.

*You're probably going to run out of foods before you ruin out of drying space with the gigantic RedHead Dehydrator. Canned pineapple rings are easy to turn into "candied" dry fruits either drained and out of the can, or by adding a few ingredients to make them crunchy, sticky, and delicious.*

# RUM PLUMS TO DRUNKEN PRUNES

- 3–5 pounds ripe plums (red or black)
- 2 cups light rum (not optional)
- 2–3 tablespoons Cajun salt/seasoning to taste
- ½–1½ teaspoons ground red pepper (optional)

Just about everyone loves fresh plums. Not everyone, however, loves them when they are dried and called "prunes." Most commercially sold prunes have little if any added flavors, and rarely taste great or anything like the original sweet summer fruits. That's all about to change with just a little rum as a marinade and a dash of some salt and heat with a little red pepper and your favorite Cajun spice!

Pit the plums and leave the skin on. Take the plum halves and marinate them overnight in a plastic bag or container in your refrigerator with the rum and Cajun salt/spice blend. If you want to make the plums a little hotter and spicier, add the optional ground red pepper. Go sparingly with this until you figure out the right combination for your taste buds. Drain and place the plums with the skin side down on the dehydrator trays and set it at 145°F. Once dried, let the *rum plums* rest and air-dry overnight before sealing them up in plastic or vacuum bags.

*Plums are super sweet and have a high moisture content. Once dried, they shrink a lot. Just make sure you make plenty for snacking.*

# CHAPTER 16

# CRUNCHY VEGGIE TRAIL SNACKS

While almost every vegetable can be successfully dehydrated, dried, and smoked (except smoked avocados), the majority of them are not on the top of the list for enjoying and eating as snacks. Dried green beans, parched corn, and crispy broccoli crowns may be great for using at home or in camp for cooking, but they're not real exciting as munchy treats.

Most veggies, unlike many fruits, can be found on a year-round basis at the supermarket, so they can be smoked or dehydrated pretty much whenever your snack stash starts to run low.

Make sure that you use a nonstick spray or wipe oil on all the dehydrator drying trays and smoker jerky racks to keep everything from sticking. Best dehydrator and electric smoker drying temperatures are around 130–135°F until the snacks are dry and very crisp. Veggies, like most fruits, are delicate when it comes to higher heats found in most propane smokers. If you are going to add a little smoke, you must keep the temperature low and well under 200°F. As an alternative, heat up the smoker and get the wood going, put the vegetables in on low temperature for only 30–45 minutes, and then move them to the dehydrator to finish off the drying process. Here is where, if you have a cold smoker, it becomes invaluable!

*Hothouse tomatoes will work, but fresh vine-ripe cherry, beefsteak and even Romas will smoke up or dehydrate deliciously with little more than your favorite Cajun or seasoning salts. Leftovers, if there are any, can even be bottled and sealed in olive oil.*

*Bell peppers (all colors) have a lot of natural sweetness that is concentrated once they are sliced and dried or smoked. They are great for trail and camp snacks. Season them up with Cajun, seasoning salt, or a splash of Worcestershire sauce and lemon pepper spice.*

# CRUNCHY SMOKED VEGETABLE MEDLEY

- 3–4 pounds Roma tomatoes
- 3–6 large bell peppers—red, green, yellow, orange
- 4–8 large sweet onions—red, white, yellow, Vidalia
- ¼ cup Hi Mountain's Cajun Campfire Sprinkles or a garlic/pepper blend with no salt
- 1–2 teaspoons ground cayenne/red pepper to taste
- ¼ cup or more Hi Mountain's Western Sizzle Steak Spice or favorite steak seasoning/rub
- 2–3 tablespoons soy sauce, Worcestershire sauce or both

This is one of those combination veggie recipes that once dried or smoked is ideal as a trail snack by itself, or can be spruced up and mixed with your favorite flavor of finely chopped jerky or bacon bits. With this recipe, you can actually make just the dried tomatoes, onions, or pepper sticks individually as snacks. Alone or together, they can also be used for cooking at home or in camp as well as preserved in a jar in olive oil.

For this recipe, we know you are going to start out with a small batch, and soon end up wanting to make more! Here is where, if you are putting up large quantities of tomatoes, you are going to want to make use of your food slicer!

Peel onion and slice for onion rings. Slice and core peppers and cut into ¾-inch lengthwise slivers. Cut tomatoes into round ⅜-inch slices. Use nonstick spray on jerky racks, then lay tomatoes out with about a ½-inch spacing between each slice, and liberally sprinkle with a garlic pepper blend and cayenne/red pepper to taste.

Take onion rings and pepper slices, put in ziplock bag, mix in a couple of big splashes of soy or Worcestershire sauce (or both), and add the Western Sizzle steak spice or seasoning salt to taste. Soy or Worcestershire coats the veggies and helps the spice adhere better. No marination time is required, and once coated, peppers and onions are ready to smoke or dry. Smoke with your favorite wood flavor at around 170°F, or dry in the dehydrator until everything is crispy and crunchy. Watch the veggies carefully in the smoker so that they do not get overcooked! If you have a cold smoke system, use it! Dehydrate at 135°F. Store the veggies in resealable plastic bags or vacuum sealed bags.

*Fruits are not the only snack treats that are seasonal. Great eating Vidalia onions seem to come and go too quickly as well. We trim up and then food-slice several big boxes each season to use in both the smokers and dehydrators. Cajun or seasoned salt is all that's needed to add great flavor.*

# SWEET SESAME VINEGAR MUSHROOMS

- 2 pounds thin sliced or stripped mushrooms
- 1 teaspoon onion powder
- 1 teaspoon garlic powder
- 4 tablespoons soy sauce
- ½ cup rice wine sake (optional)
- ½ cup rice wine vinegar or balsamic vinegar
- 2 tablespoons sesame oil
- ¼ cup canola or olive oil
- 1 teaspoon salt (sea, kosher, non-iodized, or Cajun) to taste
- 1 teaspoon minced ginger (optional)

This recipe has great flavor with just about all types of mushrooms—shiitakes, porcini, morels, chanterelles, portabellas, and even the everyday grocery store button mushroom variety. The problem with this recipe is that after marinating, it is often difficult to get them to your smoker or dehydrator. *They taste so good,* just as marinated mushrooms, watch out that they don't all disappear before you get a chance to dry or smoke them! These are great for trail snacking themselves, or added to trail mix, and can even used in home or camp cooking.

With all the ingredients mixed, marinate the mushrooms for 4–24 hours in the refrigerator. Drain and arrange on dehydrator tray and place in dryer at 130–135°F until the mushrooms are dry and crisp. Or you can throw them in the smoker with a pan or two of hickory, mesquite, or cherry wood. Cold smoking works great too!

*Fresh mushrooms—button, portabella, or whatever your favorites are—just need a bath in Worcestershire sauce and garlic salt to dry or smoke them. Add a splash or red wine or balsamic vinegar for a little extra tang.*

# LEMON SOY PORTABELLAS

- 2 pounds sliced portabella mushrooms
- ½ cup soy sauce
- 3–4 tablespoons lemon juice (fresh or bottled)
- 2 tablespoons canola or olive oil
- 3 cloves minced garlic or 2 tablespoons garlic powder

Portabella mushrooms are large, easy to slice, and have a natural earthy taste and smell. Dried after being in this marinade, they are slightly salty and lemon-tangy.

Mix ingredients and marinate for 4–24 hours. Drain and smoke with hickory, mesquite, or cherry wood. Or dehydrate at 130–135°F until dry and crisp.

*We make a lot of dehydrated and smoked mushrooms to break up and use in trail snack mixes and for camp cooking. Problem is, most all of them get eaten before they ever see the inside of a plastic or vacuum-sealed bag!*

# WESTON'S ZUCCHINI SNACK CHIPS

## Italian Style

- 1 large zucchini squash, thin chip sliced
- 2 teaspoons lemon juice
- 2 teaspoons dried basil leaves, chopped fine
- 1 teaspoon garlic powder
- 1 teaspoon oregano
- ½ teaspoon dried sage
- ¼ teaspoon black pepper
- ¼ teaspoon sea salt

## Middle Eastern Style

- 1 large zucchini squash, thin chip sliced
- 2 teaspoons lemon juice
- 2 teaspoons garam masala spice or cHarissa spice
- ½ teaspoon garlic powder
- ½ teaspoon dried mint
- ½ teaspoon red pepper
- ½ teaspoon ground coriander
- ½ teaspoon sea salt

## Spanish Style

- 1 large zucchini squash, thin chip sliced
- 1 tablespoon olive oil
- 1 tablespoon dried cilantro
- 2 teaspoons garlic powder or fresh ground
- 2 teaspoons smoked Spanish paprika
- ½ teaspoon ground cumin
- ½ teaspoon sea salt

When we first discovered all the zucchini recipes from Weston Supply (www.westonsupply. com), makers of many home dehydrators, we thought they had gone a little bit overboard! That's until we made a batch of each flavor and let everyone do a taste test. Dried in one of their dehydrators at 135°F, the crispy chips were full of flavor and a lot healthier than a handful of greasy potato chips.

Select your favorite flavor, mix ingredients, and marinate 12–24 hours in the refrigerator before drying. Don't tell the folks at Weston we told you this, but they are also excellent using the smoker and some apple or alder wood! Or they can be cold smoked before marinating and dehydrating.

*Almost all the squash varieties of veggies can be sliced, marinated, and turned into great snacks. These zucchini chips were made with the Weston Supply recipe for three different flavors. Just make plenty of each.*

# TANGY TOFU BBQ

- 14-ounce package extrafirm tofu, drained and pressed
- 2 tablespoons soy sauce
- 2 teaspoons maple syrup
- ½ teaspoon liquid smoke flavoring
- 1 teaspoon garlic powder
- ½ teaspoon ground black pepper
- 3 tablespoons barbecue sauce
- 2 teaspoons brown sugar

Just because you don't eat meat doesn't mean you can't enjoy some great homemade jerky, and at a fraction of the price for store-bought tofu products!

While tofu can be incorporated into a lot of soups, salads, and other cooked dishes, it can be also be marinated with a variety of flavors, dried/smoked, and makes a great snack for all. *Even us meat eaters!*

Firm or extrafirm tofu works best for draining, pressing, and drying. Place the tofu block between several paper towels and weight it down with a plate or fry pan. Flip the tofu, add new paper towels, and press again. Total drain/press time takes about an hour. Once drained, slice the block into ¼- to ⅜-inch slices.

Mix all ingredients together and marinate in a plastic bag or container for 12–24 hours. Drain marinade from the tofu slices and place in a 200°F home oven until it is semidry and pliable. Start checking it at around 8 hours. Tofu can also be smoked at low temperature with a pan or two of your favorite wood flavor. Hickory and mesquite will give it an earthy/bold taste, while apple or alder is a lighter and sweeter flavor. For the dehydrator, it is best at 130–145°F for 12–18 hours.

Regardless of how you are going to cook, dry, or smoke the tofu, make sure that it is checked and the slices are flipped every few hours.

*Don't let the dark color of the tofu fool you; it's not burned but marinated and smoked to perfection with a marinade combination of soy sauce and chili garlic. As the tofu smokes you can add more flavor by basting it with more soy and chili garlic.*

## SOUTH OF THE BORDER TOFU

- 14-ounce package extrafirm tofu, drained and pressed
- 1 package/envelope of grocery store taco mix blend
- 1 teaspoon rosemary
- 2 teaspoons paprika
- 1 tablespoon sugar
- 1 cup beer or water
- 2 tablespoons apple cider vinegar
- 4 tablespoons of your favorite salsa or hot sauce

A great tofu trail snack with a Mexican flavor. Take the slices along on your outdoor trip, and make sure to bring some extra hot sauce packets from the local taco stand!

Combine and puree all your marinating ingredients in the blender or food processor. Place drained ¼-inch slices of tofu in the marinade and let sit 12–24 hours in the refrigerator. Drain and dehydrate dry at 130–145°F until tofu is bendable and pliable. Keep flipping and turning every few hours.

## HOISIN AND HOT TOFU

- 14-ounce package extrafirm tofu, drained and pressed
- 2 tablespoons red wine vinegar
- ¼ cup soy sauce
- 1 cup beer or water
- ¾–1 cup hoisin (Chinese BBQ sauce)
- 3–4 tablespoons sriracha hot chili sauce

Hoisin sauce is often called Chinese BBQ sauce here in America. It's sweet and tangy, and gives tofu a BBQed flavor when dry. Heat levels for your taste buds can be adjusted up or down with the sriracha hot chili sauce, and as the tofu dries, you can lightly baste on more to your tastes.

Combine ¼-inch thick tofu slices with the marinade ingredients, let sit in the refrigerator for 12–24 hours, then dehydrate dry at 130–145°F until tofu is bendable and pliable.

# AVOCADO CHIPS

- 4 avocados, peeled and sliced to ¼-inch thickness
- 2–3 tablespoons lemon juice—fresh
- 1 teaspoon lemon zest
- ¼ cup fresh cilantro
- ¼ teaspoon cayenne pepper
- ¼ teaspoon Cajun or seasoning salt

Avocados are actually a fruit, even though most folks think they are a veggie. Avocado chips made in the dehydrator are great for snacking by themselves, or are something different as a replacement for potato chips and served with your favorite dip—ranch, French onion, salsa, etc. This recipe from Weston Supply (www.westonsupply.com) works great for what many call alligator pears and makes them ideal for dehydrating. However, avocados are absolutely the worst thing you've tasted when you try to smoke them! For whatever reason, *they suck!*

With this marinade and a few hours in the refrigerator, they can be dried at about 165°F for 9–12 hours. Remove them from the dehydrator when crispy and crunchy. And remember, don't try to smoke them!

*Avocado or alligator pears can be seasoned up with your favorite spices and dehydrated at low temperatures (130°F) until they turn into flavorful chips. If they are smoked and dried, they turn out bitter and terrible!*

# CHAPTER 17

# TREMENDOUS TRAIL SNACKS—MEATS, TREATS, NUTS, AND SWEETS

*Man should not live by jerky alone!* Neither should women, kids, or all your friends. . . .

As you will soon discover, your home oven, smoker, and dehydrator can also be used to make a host of home, camp, and trail foods that are easy to prepare, affordable, and are going to become everyone's favorites.

*Canned or bottled almonds are boring and expensive! Make you own in the dehydrator or smoker. They can be smoked and salty (left) or dehydrated with cinnamon and sugar for a sweet treat (right).*

# KAT'S SIMPLE SUMMER SAUSAGES

## Garlic Pepper Blend

- 3 pounds ground meat (beef is good, but big game is best)
- 1 cup beer or water
- 3 tablespoons curing salt
- 1 tablespoon mustard seeds
- 1 teaspoon fresh ground black pepper
- 1 teaspoon whole peppercorns
- 1 tablespoon fresh chopped garlic
- 2 teaspoons liquid smoke flavoring
- ½ teaspoon onion powder

## Italian Blend

Kathy Mattoon (author) has been making this dry summer sausage for over twenty years, and has a long list of recipients that are always begging for more! The original recipe comes from Oklahoma and dates back nearly fifty years. It is easy to make, and really brings out the flavor with any big game ground meats. As a last resort and if your freezer is bare, *you can, if you have to, use beef!*

*Same ingredients as above, but add:*
- 1 tablespoon oregano
- 1 teaspoon rosemary
- 1 teaspoon thyme
- 1 tablespoon basil
- 1 teaspoon marjoram

Mix all spices together and add the ground meat. Blend thoroughly and divide into five equal rolls. Wrap in foil and refrigerate 24 hours to let everything blend together. Finish off in the oven at 300°F for 1½ hours, or the smoker (300°F) with hickory wood, or for a sweeter taste try, apple wood.

   As a final option to your creativity, you can also add to the meat blend—chopped jalapeños, black/green olives, mushrooms, cheese, onions, bell peppers, or even sweet and dill pickles.

*Cured ground meats for summer sausage are wrapped up in aluminum foil and readied for the home oven or smoker. If you are going to smoke the rolls, go easy on the liquid smoke flavoring and let them smoke naturally with mesquite, hickory, or cherry wood.*

# BBQ LUNCH MEAT ROLLUPS

- 2 pounds pre-sliced lunch meats (ham, turkey, pastrami roast beef, chicken or whatever your favorites are)
- ¾ cup hoisin sauce (Chinese BBQ)
- ¼ cup soy sauce
- 1 teaspoon garlic powder
- 1 teaspoon onion powder
- 2–4 tablespoons hot sauce (Tabasco, Louisiana, or sriracha)

This is one of those recipes that is so simple we can't believe that one of the giant lunch meat companies is not already marketing it! You simply use either prepacked sliced luncheon meats or have your store's deli counter thin slice up what you need.

For trail snacking, it saves having to worry about refrigerating lunch and snack meats, and with the additional flavor combinations it is fast and easy finger food.

Mix all ingredients but the meats. Spread lunch meats flat and use a basting brush to paint the meats with the flavor mixture. Roll up and pin with a toothpick, and let marinate in the refrigerator for a couple of hours. Dehydrate at 145–155°F until the meat has dried and will bend but not break. Remove the toothpicks and store in ziplock or vacuum sealed bags.

*Harissa is a spice and seasoning rub from North Africa that you can make at home and adds a very different and distinct tastes to meat, poultry, and fish jerky. The cHarissa prepackaged spice rubs (Original and With a Kick) offer the same type of great flavor.*

# SPICY TERIYAKI SPAM STEAK

- 1–2 cans of Spam, sliced ¼- to ⅜-inch thick
- 1 cup teriyaki sauce
- ½ cup beer or water
- 2 tablespoons ground red pepper or flakes

Yes, we know that not everyone is a Spam fan. Much maligned since WWII when it was first introduced, it still rates as the best-selling canned meat in all of Hawaii, and there are actually many restaurants that have Spam on their menus! The name Spam is a shortened version of "spiced ham" and it seems to be one of those meats that you either love or hate.

Mix your spices together and marinate the slices for 12–24 hours in your refrigerator. It can be dehydrated until bendable/pliable at 145–155°F, or it's even better when put in the smoker at around 200°F and smoked with several pans of hickory or mesquite woods.

*Coming out of the can, Spam may not be everyone's favorite. Once sliced and spiced up, they are a favorite for the smoker with your favorite wood flavor or oven dried. Trust us . . . you really are going to enjoy them!*

# HOT DOG SWEET HEAT SNACKS

- 1 pound all beef hot dogs, quartered lengthwise
- 1 cup teriyaki sauce
- 3 tablespoons honey or maple syrup
- 1 teaspoon liquid smoke flavoring (optional)

Turning your favorite all-beef hot dog into a dried and delicious meat snack is another one of those easy-to-prepare trail sticks that are great for camping or when munching on the trail.

Quarter the hot dogs lengthwise and mix with the teriyaki and honey or maple syrup blend. Add the mesquite or hickory liquid smoke flavoring if you want that flavor and allow to marinate 12–24 hours. Even hot dogs take time to absorb the flavors. Drain and finish the dogs off in the dehydrator at 145–155°F until they are semidry and pliable. If you are going to use the smoker, keep the temp around 175°F and use mesquite or hickory woods.

*Believe it or not, all-beef hot dogs when quartered lengthwise and marinated in your own cure, or even with commercial blends, can be turned into great smoked trail snacks. Smokehouse's Black Pepper and Hi Mountain Seasonings's Jalapeño were two of the top favorites.*

# COLD SMOKE CAMP CHEESE

- 2–5 pounds sliced or chunked hard cheese—cheddar, cheese balls, Swiss, pepper jack, mozzarella, etc.
- 1 jar jalapeño jelly (optional)
- ⅓ cup Cajun season salt (optional)

It is simple to take a brick of cheese, slice it, spice it, smoke it up, and transform *a bland $3–4 hunk of cheese* into a $15 special treat that everyone is going to want on your next outdoor adventure. If you share with your friends, don't be surprised if they show up soon with armfuls of cheap cheese and ask about using your cold smoker and gourmet techniques. We even smoked a "cheapy" store-bought cheese ball and turned it into a delicious ball of *smokiness* that had to be hidden away in our fishing camp!

After slicing the brick cheeses, and leaving the cheese ball whole, we converted our old propane BBQ grill into an instant "cold smoker" with the electric *Smoke Chief* from Smokehouse Products (www.smokehouseproducts.com). Cheeses were generously basted with the mix of jalapeño jelly and Cajun salt seasoning, and placed in the freezer to harden up before being cold smoked for about 4 hours with apple wood pellets.

The other way to cold smoke your cheese and avoid everything melting into a gooey mess is to use your smoker and keep the temperature low, low, low. Again, freeze your cheeses and try to keep the smoker temperature below 175°F after the wood starts to smoke. Prop the door open and keep in mind that you want lots of smoke and as little heat as possible.

If you are hard-core about doing a lot of cold smoking for cheeses, eggs, nuts, fruits, fish, cured meats, veggies, and more, take a look at the *Cold Smoker* attachment that hooks onto several models of the grills from Traeger Wood Pellet Grills (www.traegergrills.com). It gives you the smoke, and you can manage the heat to less than 175°F.

*Almost all the flavorful hard cheese types can be sliced or chunked and smoked for a real gourmet treat. If you do not have a cold smoke system, try freezing the cheese slices before putting them into the smoker and keeping the smoke high and the temperatures low.*

# PEANUT BUTTER & JELLY ROLLUPS

- 1 23-ounce jar of blackberry, strawberry, or your favorite jam flavor
- ¼ cup apple juice
- 1–2 cups peanut butter

So who doesn't love an iconic PB&J sandwich? With this recipe you can make it in fruit leather form to take on the trail or for long-term storage in the refrigerator or freezer. The kids will love them, but . . . so do we!

Put the jam and apple juice in a blender or food processor. When nice and smooth, pour onto an oiled solid-plastic dehydrator tray. Set the dryer at 130°F and start checking for dryness after about eight hours. When dry like leather, spread your favorite peanut butter on top, roll it up, and cut into bite-size pieces. Bites store well in refrigerator or freezer.

*Take your favorite jelly or jam and blend with apple juice or applesauce till smooth and creamy. Dry in the dehydrator at 135-145°F until the mixture turns solid, but pliable. Smear peanut butter over the leather . . . and you have an instant PB&J treat.*

# PEACHY APRICOT PIE ROLLUP

- 1 can peaches, drained
- 1 can apricots, drained
- ¼ cup brown sugar
- 1 tablespoon lime juice (fresh or bottled)
- 1–2 tablespoons rum (light or dark)
- ½ teaspoon cinnamon
- ¼ teaspoon ground nutmeg
- ½ teaspoon vanilla (pure or extract)

It's a fruit leather or rollup, but it tastes exactly like a combination peach and apricot pie. Mix and blend all ingredients in a blender or food processor until nice and smooth. Pour the mix onto an oiled/nonstick-sprayed solid-plastic dehydrator tray. Set the dehydrator at 130°F and start checking for that semi-dried leathery texture in about 8 hours.

*Peaches can be dehydrated or lightly smoked with or without their skins left on. Sliced to ¼ of an inch in thickness, you can top them off before drying/smoking with a light sprinkle of blended sugar and cinnamon.*

# PUMPKIN PIE LEATHER

- 1 can pumpkin meat
- 1 tablespoon pumpkin pie spice
- 1 cup apple juice
- ½ cup brown sugar
- ½ cup apple sauce

So who says you have to wait for Thanksgiving or Christmas to enjoy pumpkin pie? Instead you can make it year-round as a trail and camp snack and simply call it dessert!

Put all your ingredients in the blender or food processor; process until smooth. Pour onto oiled solid-dehydrator trays that are designed for making rollups, to a depth of about ¼ inch. Dehydrate at 130–135°F and start checking for it to be solid but pliable after about 6–8 hours. Remove from dryer, cut into small strips, and roll them up.

*The pumpkins may not be happy about it, but using canned pumpkin meat and turning it into fruit leather strips is a great way to enjoy that holiday pie flavor on a year-round basis.*

*Banana fruit rollups are easy with a few simple flavor ingredients. If you want to take it up in the taste deparment, add crushed walnuts to the banana and applesauce mix before putting it in your dehydrator. Leather should be firm, flexible, but not sticky.*

# BANANA NUT BREAD LEATHER

- 4 ripe to slightly overripe bananas
- 1–1½ tablespoons vanilla (extract or pure)
- 1 cup brown sugar
- ½ cup or more finely chopped walnuts, pecans, or almonds

Easier and a lot less time-consuming than making the real homemade banana bread, but the taste is the same. It is a great one to surprise your family and friends by just adding the fresh chopped nuts.

Put all the ingredients in blender or food processor (except the nuts) and blend until smooth. Pour out on an oiled solid dehydrator tray designed for making fruit leather to a depth of about ¼ inch. Sprinkle liberally with your favorite chopped nuts. Put in the dehydrator at 130–135°F for about 8 hours, give or take. When done cut into squares or strips to roll up, and just watch them disappear. They can also be garnished with a light sprinkle of powdered sugar. Next time, you'll want to double or triple the recipe.

# STRAWBERRIES 'N CREAM ROLLUP

- 2 cups strawberries (fresh, canned, or frozen)
- ½ cup sugar
- ½ cup whipping cream
- Applesauce if needed for consistency

Blend strawberries, sugar, and whipping cream until smooth. You want to blend/puree it to the consistency of applesauce. If you need to add a little applesauce that's okay. Just add a little at a time, and don't overdo it.

Spread out on sprayed or oiled solid dehydrator tray ¼ thick. Put into dehydrator at 130°F for about 8 hours until it's pliable and not sticky. Roll up and cut into pieces, put in a ziplock bag, and refrigerate or freeze.

*If you can grow your own raspberries, consider yourself lucky. Dried in the dehydrator or processed in a blender with some applesauce, you can make your own healthy fruit leather rollups.*

# WESTON'S FRUIT LEATHERS

## Raspberry Vanilla

- 1 pint raspberries (fresh or frozen)
- Seeds of 1 vanilla bean
- ¼ cup honey

## Blueberry Apple Ginger

- ¼ cup blueberries (fresh or frozen)
- 3 large Red Delicious apples, peeled, sliced, and cored
- 1½ teaspoons grated ginger root
- ¾ cup sugar
- 1 tablespoon lemon juice

## Strawberry Rhubarb

- 4 cups strawberries (fresh or frozen), hulled
- 2 cups rhubarb
- 2 cups superfine sugar
- 1 tablespoon fresh lemon juice

## Mixed Berry

- 1 pint blackberries (fresh or frozen)
- 1 pint blueberries (fresh or frozen)
- 1 pint strawberries (fresh or frozen)
- 1½ cups superfine sugar
- 1 tablespoon fresh lemon juice

All of these recipes from Weston Supply (www.westonsupply.com) are pretty simple and straightforward. Once your ingredients are all pureed in the blender or food processor, simply fill your solid dehydrator tray or wax paper–lined tray with the mix to no more than ¼ inch deep. Turn up your Weston dehydrator at around 135°F, and dehydrate until the liquid dries up and it becomes that fruit leather texture. Start checking after around 8 hours of drying time. Slice as snacks or roll up into bites. Bites store well in the refrigerator or freezer.

*Blueberries dry up crisp and crunchy and they also lightly smoke well. If you want to "crack" the tough outer skins, simply drop them in boiling water for 30 seconds and then move them to a bath of ice water.*

# DRIED YOGURT CHIPS

- 3–6 single serve yogurt cups or more
- 2 tablespoons powdered sugar (optional)
- ⅓–½ cup dried and chopped fruits—raisins, blueberries, apricots, pineapple, peach, kiwi, or your favorite chopped nuts!

With this recipe you will be glad you have a large capacity dehydrator. Simply spoon out small dollops of your favorite flavored yogurt onto an oiled/nonstick sprayed solid dehydrator tray, sprinkle a little powdered sugar on each for added sweetness, and then top them off with a little piece of your favorite fruit or sprinkled with chopped nuts!

Dry in the dehydrator at 135–145°F, until the yogurt chips become crispy and crunchy. *They are not going to last long!*

# RED HOT APPLE CINNAMON SNACKS

- 1 24-ounce jar of applesauce
- 1 box red hot cinnamon candies
- 1–2 teaspoons ground cinnamon or to taste

No blender or food processer needed here. Just spread the applesauce out on a oiled, solid dehydrator sheet to a depth of about ¼ inch. Sprinkle the candies and cinnamon on top and put in dehydrator at 135°F for about 8 hours. Dry until it is pliable and not tacky.

*All the apple pie rollup (left) needs is a dab of whipped cream. The Hot Tamales or Red Hots candy rollup (right) gives the basic apple pie treat a little cinnamon heat. Both store well in plastic bags in your refrigerator or freezer.*

# CATSUP LEATHERS

- 1 large bottle catsup
- 1–2 tablespoons fresh ground black pepper (optional)
- 1 tablespoon garlic powder (optional)
- 1–2 tablespoons Cajun seasoning salt (optional)

If you've ever lugged in your backpack a large bottle of catsup into your hunting or fishing camp, you know it tips the scales at 2½ pounds. Dehydrate it and you can reduce it to a mere 6–8 ounces!

Simply add pepper, garlic, and Cajun salt to kick up the flavor profile, or squirt it right out of the bottle onto an oiled solid dehydrator tray to a depth of about ¼ inch. Dehydrate at 135°F for about 8 hours and make sure it's pliable and not sticky. Cut the leather into squares separated by plastic wrap, and then seal in a ziplock or vacuum-sealed bag. It is awesome on hamburgers, can be used as a wrap around jerky or meat sticks, and can even be reconstituted in a pan with a little water for camp cooking!

*Plain old bottled catsup can be dried in your dehydrator and made into a vegetable leather. The dried squares are great for wrapping around a jerky strip or ground meat snackin' stick, or used in camp cooking.*

# SPAGHETTI SAUCE LEATHER SNACKS

- 1 large jar or can of your favorite spaghetti sauce
- ¼ cup grated Parmesan or Romano cheese, grated fine (optional)

This is one of those insanely easy and delicious recipes that you can use for trail snacking or camp cooking. It also eliminates virtually all the weight of trying to pack in a large jar of spaghetti sauce.

Just take your bottle of spaghetti sauce and spread it out on sprayed or oiled solid dehydrator rack/sheet. Spread it out to no more than ¼ inch thick and place in the dehydrator at 135°F for around 8 hours. It's ready to bag or munch on with dried veggies or jerky snacks when it is pliable and not sticky. And yes, with a little water, it can be reconstituted and used for cooking.

*Any large jar of spaghetti sauce can be thrown in your dehydrator and turned into a dried leather that can be used for camp cooking or trail snacking. Make sure that you use a dryer rack designed for liquids, and give it a good shot of nonstick spray before spreading.*

# HICKORY SMOKED ALMONDS

- 3 cups unblanched/raw almonds
- 2 teaspoons garlic powder
- ¼–½ teaspoon salt or seasoned salt
- 2 teaspoons celery salt
- ½ teaspoon liquid smoke
- 1–2 egg whites

While raw almonds aren't cheap, they're a heck of lot less expensive than those store-bought "cans." This is one of those recipes that we suggest you start with 3 cups of almonds, but we can guarantee that you will wish you doubled or tripled the recipe. *They never last long!*

Whisk the egg white in a bowl until foamy. Add the spices and blend thoroughly. Add the almonds and mix until the nuts are well coated. Spread out on a cooking spray–coated baking pan or fine-mesh jerky rack. Nuts can be oven baked at 300°F for about 30 minutes, stirring every 10 minutes. Or, they can go into the smoker at 300°F with a pan or two of hickory or mesquite wood. Nuts will be soft when removed from heat, so allow to air-dry. Be careful not to overcook/heat or they will have a burnt, rancid flavor.

*Almonds can be dried or smoked, and either made salty with a little seasoning, or made into sweet treats with a little sugar.*

# SMOKY CHEX MIX

- 3 cups Corn Chex
- 3 cups Rice Chex
- 3 cups Wheat Chex
- 1 cup smoked almonds
- 1 cup salted/roasted peanuts
- 1 cup mini pretzels
- 6 tablespoons butter
- 2 tablespoons Worcester shire sauce
- 1 teaspoon liquid smoke flavoring
- 1½ teaspoons Cajun or seasoned salt
- ¾ teaspoon garlic powder
- 1 teaspoon onion powder
- 1–2 cups dried chopped fruit
- 1 cup chopped/shredded jerky (whatever your favorite flavors are)

*Your homemade Chex Mix is a great trail snack by itself, but you can really make it a nutritious treat by adding chopped bits of jerky and dried fruits.*

This favorite trail, camp, and home snack mix has been around forever and is easy to make. Making fresh is a lot cheaper than buying the ready-made stuff at the grocery store. We love to add dried fruit pieces and small chunks or shreds of several different dried jerky bites.

In a large microwave-safe bowl, combine cereals, nuts, and pretzels and set aside. In small microwaveable bowl, microwave the butter, Worcester shire sauce, liquid smoke, and spices uncovered for about 20–30 seconds. Pour over cereal mixture; stir until evenly coated. Microwave uncovered on high for 4–6 minutes, thoroughly stirring 1–2 minutes. Spread out on paper towels or jerky rack to cool. Store the mix in an airtight container.

If you are going to use the home oven, set it to 250°F. Bake 1 hour, stirring every 15 minutes. Spread on paper towel cool. And if you want real smoke flavor, get your smoker up to 250°F with a large pan of your favorite wood flavor. We found hickory wood to be big and bold! Bake/smoke for 1 hour, stirring every 10–15 minutes.

# ROSEMARY CASHEWS

- 2–3 cups cashews
- 3 tablespoons unsalted butter, melted
- ¼ cup fresh rosemary needles, chopped
- 1 teaspoon Traeger Cajun Rub, or substitute Cajun salt
- ½ teaspoon cayenne pepper

The folks at Traeger Wood Pellet Grills (www.traegergrills.com) say that these cashews will have a hard time ever being bagged up for very long!

Once everything is mixed together, and you are ready to start cooking/smoking. Spread the mix onto a large pan, get your grill or smoker up to 350°F, and bake/cook/smoke for 10–12 minutes. Stir occasionally and remove when the cashews begin to toast.

*Smoked rosemary cashews from the folks at Traeger Wood Pellet Grills are a quick and easy way to give the nuts a rosemary-sweet and salty flavor with a little Cajun heat. Just 10–12 minutes in the smoker at 350°F is all that's needed.*

# SMOKY PUMPKIN SEEDS

- 3–5 cups pumpkin seeds (salvage them from leftover Halloween pumpkin carvings)
- 2 cups warm water
- ¼ cup Cajun seasoning salt
- 1–2 teaspoons liquid smoke flavoring

Every year, we can't wait for the Halloween season to come, and everyone starts selling pumpkins that are loaded up with seeds and ready to be carved. But instead of buying the pumpkins before Halloween, we wait until the day after and head to the grocery store to see about all their leftovers. *Oftentimes you can buy a trunk load of leftovers for pennies on the dollar.*

Cut the pumpkins open, remove all the seeds, and wash thoroughly. Place seeds in the warm water, seasoned salt, and liquid smoke mixture, blend well, and let marinate for a few hours. Drain seeds, spread them out, and let them air-dry. You can add additional Cajun seasoning salt or sprinkle ground red pepper to kick the flavor up a couple of notches!

Regardless of how you are going to dry or smoke the seeds, make sure that you stir and flip them often. Seeds can be placed in the dehydrator at 135–145°F until dried completely. If you are going to use the home oven, 200°F on a cookie sheet is your best bet until dry. For the smoker, spread them out on a tight-mesh jerky rack and smoke/dry at 200°F with a couple of pans of hickory or mesquite.

Store in sealed canning jars, plastic bags, or containers. You're going to wish that pumpkins were available year-round, or that you bought a lot more when they went on sale!

*Pumpkins purchased after Halloween are often available for pennies on the dollar! Seeds can be smoked at low temperature with mesquite wood, or oven-dried. Add a little liquid smoke to your salted water give them even more flavor.*

# PINEAPPLE CANDY

- 1 large can sliced pineapple, or substitute fresh sliced
- 1½ cups water
- ½ cup sugar
- 1 teaspoon lemon juice (fresh or bottled)

Mix the blend together and bring to a boil. Add the pineapple rings and boil for 10 minutes. Reduce heat to medium and let simmer for 30 minutes. Liquid should thicken and will become very syrupy.

Remove from stove and allow the slices to cool while you apply nonstick spray or oil to your dehydrator trays. Once cooled, remove slices from liquid and dry in the dehydrator at 135°F until the slices are firm, pliable, and not tacky.

*Fresh or even canned pineapple can be dried or lightly smoked for a great trail snack. If you want your pineapple strips turned into a "candy treat," simply use the strips and don't add anything.*

# CRYSTALLIZED MINT LEAF/FLOWER CANDY

- 1 large bunch of mint leaves or edible flower petals
- 2–3 egg whites
- 1 dash of salt
- ¼ cup or more, powdered sugar

If you grow spearmint, peppermint, nasturtiums, pansies, or Johnny-jump-ups in your yard, you've got the basics for some great and unusual homemade candy that is very easy to make.

Use fresh and healthy looking mint leaves or edible flowers. Wash thoroughly and allow to air-dry. Take the egg whites and beat/whip until foamy. Add a dash of salt to help break up the egg whites while beating. Take the foamy egg white and use a basting brush to paint the mint leaves or flowers. Or simply take the petals or mint leaves and dip them in the eggs. Lay petals/leaves on fine mesh dehydrator racks and sprinkle liberally with white powdered sugar.

Dehydrate at low temperature, just 100–110°F, until the petals and leaves become crisp. Once dried, they literally become an exotic melt-in-your-mouth candy treat.

*Edible flower petals and fresh mint leaves are a melt-in-your-mouth treat, literally. Egg white–washed and then sprinkled with powdered sugar, they go into the dehydrator at 100-110°F until crisp.*

# INDEX